How Energy Affects the Economy

How Energy Affects the Economy

Edited by
A. Bradley Askin

Lexington Books
D. C. Heath and Company
Lexington, Massachusetts
Toronto

Library of Congress Cataloging in Publication Data

Main entry under title:

How energy affects the economy.

    1. Energy policy—United States—Addresses, essays, lectures. 2. United States—Economic conditions—1971—Addresses, essays, lectures. 3. Economic forecasting—United States—Addresses, essays, lectures. I. Askin, A. Bradley.
HD9501.U52H68   330.9'73'092   77-70084
ISBN 0-669-01365-X

Published simultaneously in Canada

Printed in the United States of America

International Standard Book Number: 0-669-01365-X

Library of Congress Catalog Card Number: 77-70084
78-6579

To Len and Hilda,
without whose parentage this
book would have been neither
possible nor necessary.

Contents

List of Figures

List of Tables

xi

Preface

The project to prepare this book was undertaken for three reasons. First, despite a rapidly growing literature on the energy problem and the economics of energy, relatively little has appeared on the relationships between the energy sector and the general economy. It was thought that this collection of papers could make a modest contribution in this area. Second, work on the topic undertaken at the Federal Energy Administration (FEA) has not been widely disseminated. It was hoped that this volume would make work done at the FEA more accessible to individuals outside the federal energy bureaucracy and encourage them to use it, critically evaluate it, and improve on it. Third, all of the contributors to the book were anxious to see their words in print and become famous or notorious as fate may have it.

Some of the papers presented in this book are the direct outgrowth of FEA analyses. Others represent spin-offs of such analyses or the contributors' research efforts conducted late at night. All of the papers are published here for the first time in their present form. Previous versions of Chapters 5 and 8 were presented at conferences, however, and the earlier version of Chapter 5 did appear in a conference proceedings volume. All of the contributors bear a debt to the FEA for services provided in support of their efforts and gratefully acknowledge the assistance, both moral and substantive, provided by colleagues and superiors. At the same time, the usual caveats hold: the views and opinions expressed in this book are those of the individual contributors and do not necessarily represent the official, or unofficial, policies of the FEA or the government.

Brenda Lelansky performed exceptional secretarial work in typing the final manuscript and multiple drafts of most chapters while the contributors and editor got their acts together as much as possible. Helen Alston, Neva Harrison, Deborah McGee, and Helen Taylor provided valued support in typing drafts of selected chapters. The contributors have unanimously requested that all errors be attributed to the editor, who has decided to retaliate by limiting his research to motorcycling and sailing for the next several months.

A. Bradley Askin
June 1977

How Energy Affects the Economy

1
The Dilemmas of Setting Energy Policy
A. Bradley Askin

In late 1973, the Arab members of the Organization of Petroleum Exporting Countries (OPEC) imposed an oil embargo on the United States. That act led to a growing and widespread concern about the energy problems facing the United States among politicians and other decision-makers in the public sector, vested interests in the private sector, and the general public. Are the energy problems real and serious? What are the nature and dimensions of such problems? How can they be solved? What constitutes appropriate policy responses?

On October 17, 1973, the Arab members of OPEC met to discuss the outbreak of war between Egypt and Israel. In the following two weeks, they joined together in announcing crude oil production cut-backs and bans on all petroleum shipments to the United States and the Netherlands. Although the embargo lasted only until March 17, 1974, and did not significantly interrupt U.S. oil imports, it did result in a permanent quadrupling of OPEC crude oil prices and impose a psychological shock that focused attention on the "energy crisis."

Once the energy crisis hit, the relatively arcane subject of energy became a topic of widespread interest overnight. It quickly became the conventional wisdom that swift, forceful public action was needed before the United States either ran out of energy or became excessively dependent on foreign sources of energy. However, a consensus has yet to form on what that public action should be. On the one hand, it has been argued that government regulation of energy markets is needed to counteract years of shifting and ineffective public policy, restore competition in energy markets, and protect consumers. Many forms of such regulation have been proposed, including the program President Carter sent to Congress in April 1977. On the other hand, it has been argued that government regulation itself is the source of the problem and must be reformed or terminated. Many versions of such reform or termination have also been suggested, including the oil decontrol proposals of President Ford.[a]

One reason that agreement has not yet been reached about the proper course of public action is that energy policy has been asked to achieve many different goals. For example, the Federal Energy Administration (FEA) implicitly proposed at least eight objectives for energy policy in its *Project Independence*

---

[a]Government regulation of energy markets goes back at least fifty years to the enactment of state prorationing laws in the 1920s. See [5, pp. 72-76]. For a description of the energy program President Carter sent to Congress, see [1]. Askin and Farman discuss the oil decontrol proposals of President Ford in Chapter 5 of this volume.

1

Report: energy autarky; positive, or at least the absence of negative, impacts on the economy; insulation of low income households from increases in energy costs; minimal regional disparities related to the availability or cost of energy supplies; minimal degradation of the environmental; minimal governmental intervention; low and stable energy prices; and preservation of domestic energy resources.[b]

Many of these energy policy objectives conflict with one another. Viewed as criteria for choosing among energy policies, they imply multiple rankings of policies depending on the importance attached to individual objectives.[c] Consider the policy of promoting energy autarky by letting domestic energy prices rise in order to encourage domestic energy production and discourage energy consumption. Rising energy prices would lead to inflation, the likelihood of reduced economic growth, and increased energy costs for consumers at all income levels. Moreover, increasing domestic energy production would degrade the environment and use up nonrenewable energy resources. Implementation of regulations to avoid some of these effects would increase government intervention and have other undesirable consequences.

Several of the objectives for energy policy proposed by the FEA involve the macroeconomic effects of energy events. Unfortunately, while economists have undertaken a significant amount of policy-directed energy analysis, the majority of it until quite recently has focused on microeconomic issues.[d] As a result, much remains unknown about the way alternative energy policies would affect the economy. This lack of information is a second reason for the lack of agreement about the course of public action that should be adopted with respect to energy policy.

Currently available models provide an incomplete, often incorrect, specification of the quantitative relationships between the energy sector and the economy in general. On the one hand, energy sector models developed to treat interfuel substitution realistically have taken the rest of the economy as given. On the other hand, income determination models, regional economic models, and consumer behavior models have not considered the energy sector in sufficient detail, when they have considered it at all, to differentiate among fuel-specific energy events. Therefore, quantitative macroeconomic assessments of

---

[b]See [3, pp. 18–20].

[c]For a more extensive treatment of the conflicts among energy policy objectives, leading to what the author thinks is the proper resolution, see [4].

[d]Up to the last few years, economists have been more interested in econometric energy demand and supply studies, institutional analysis of competition in the world petroleum market, derivations of optimal control rules for depleting nonrenewable resources, evaluations of vertical divestiture in the domestic oil industry, and the like, than in constructing models of the relationship between the energy sector and the economy in general.

various energy policies have had to rely on successive applications of energy sector models and other models, adding model incompatibility and inconsistency errors to the errors inherent in the individual models. Improved specification of the quantitative relationship between the energy sector and the economy in general using new, necessarily complex models is vital for understanding completely and precisely the macroeconomic implications of alternative energy policies. Until such improved models are operational, however, there is little alternative to using existing models as carefully as possible.

This book presents a series of policy-oriented studies on the relationship between the energy sector and the economy in general. Although an attempt is made in all of the studies to explain the methodologies used, the aim of the book is to provide insight into the ways energy events and policies affect the economy. Accordingly, discussions of econometric and modelling issues have been intentionally limited. The studies fall into two categories. Chapters 2 through 5 consider the effects of recent energy events and policy actions taken in response to those events. Chapters 6 through 10 consider the implications of a common set of energy scenarios for 1985.

In Chapter 2, David E. Serot analyzes the role that the 1973-1974 energy crisis played in the 1974-1975 recession. He reviews the evidence from earlier studies, examines the behavior of aggregate demand in the private economy, and assesses fiscal and monetary policy. Serot concludes that the energy crisis made the recession worse, but did not single-handedly cause it.

In Chapter 3, William G. Rice and Eugene Rossidivito investigate energy consumption patterns in U.S. manufacturing during the period from 1967 to 1974. They find that consumption patterns were stable in manufacturing as a whole and some major energy-consuming industries, but shifted in other major energy-consuming industries. They show that rising energy prices offer a plausible, if tentative, explanation for the shifts that occurred.

In Chapter 4, Peter Morici, Jr., surveys the impacts of higher oil prices on the Western industrial economies, including the United States. He considers the theoretical impacts of higher energy prices in general, reviews recent empirical work on the impacts of the crude oil price increases that accompanied and followed the 1973-1974 energy crisis, and briefly summarizes the long-term impacts that are likely.

In Chapter 5, A. Bradley Askin and Richard L. Farman examine the effects that the pricing provisions of the Energy Policy and Conservation Act of 1975 and the Energy Conservation and Production Act of 1976 can be expected to have on energy independence and the national economy over the next few years if not superseded by new legislation. They employ simulations of an FEA energy model and a macroeconometric model to evaluate six different crude oil pricing schemes. Askin and Farman report that the alternative pricing regimes have only minor effect on energy imports, inflation, or real output.

In Chapter 6, Arthur J. Malloy forecasts the level of economic activity in

1985 for fourteen alternative energy scenarios with the long-term Wharton model. He describes the methodology used, discusses its weaknesses, and then turns to an explanation of the different macroeconomic futures that the alternative scenarios imply. Malloy concludes that these futures are consistent with theoretical expectations.

In Chapter 7, Farman and Gerard L. Lagace use the Data Resources, Inc. (DRI) model to forecast the level of economic activity in 1985 for thirteen of the scenarios considered by Malloy. They describe their methodology, explain its limitations, and present their empirical results. They find energy price changes to have larger effects than energy policy changes, but caution that this outcome is at least partly preordained by the structure of the DRI model.

In Chapter 8, Askin compares the Malloy and Farman-Lagace analyses. After summarizing the two methodologies and their problems, he undertakes a review of their results. Discovering differences between the two sets of results, he extends both methodologies in an effort to reconcile the studies, but without success.

In Chapter 9, Ronald F. Earley and Malek M. Mohtadi consider the sector and occupation employment implications of the Farman-Lagace macroeconomic analysis. Using a 129 sector input-output model and a highly disaggregated occupation matrix, they use nineteen components of final demand forecasted by Farman-Lagace to project employment levels in 1985 for each scenario. Earley and Mohtadi discover that changes in energy prices and policies cause sector and occupation employment levels to shift in complex, nonadditive fashion.

In Chapter 10, A. David Sandoval and Robert M. Schnapp investigate the regional earnings implications of selected energy scenarios using a recursive system of linked models. They look at changes in energy prices and policies with two different versions of this system and obtain similar results with each version. Sandoval and Schnapp find that energy events affect regional earnings in complicated, but explainable ways.

Table 1-1 summarizes the main features of the 1985 energy scenarios considered in Chapters 6 through 10. Analyzed with the Project Independence Evaluation System (PIES), the scenarios combine assumptions about the world price of crude oil with assumptions about domestic energy policy. The prices in the *National Energy Outlook* scenario names indicate the assumed world price of crude oil in 1975 dollars, the year those scenarios were developed. The prices in the *Project Independence Report* scenario names indicate the assumed world price of crude oil in 1973 dollars, the year those scenarios were developed.[e]

The Reference and Business as Usual scenarios assume a continuation of present energy policies. The Conservation scenarios assume a full set of actions that reduce the demand for energy, including automobile efficiency standards, van pooling, thermal and appliance efficiency standards, accelerated industrial

---

[e]See [2] and [3].

Table 1-1
PIES Energy Projections for 1985

	Gross Energy Consumption in Quadrillions of Btu	Net Energy Consumption in Quadrillions of Btu	Energy Imports in Quadrillions of Btu	Average Price of Energy Per Btu in 1975 Dollars
National Energy Outlook Scenarios				
Reference $8	103.4	80.6	30.0	$2.59
Reference $13	98.9	75.8	13.8	3.20
Reference $16	97.3	74.0	8.3	3.53
Conservation $8	96.8	74.4	23.4	2.44
Conservation $13	93.0	70.3	9.3	3.09
Conservation $16	92.5	69.4	3.8	3.35
Accelerated Supply $8	105.2	82.3	22.6	2.45
Accelerated Supply $13	101.8	78.4	5.0	2.94
Accelerated Supply $16	101.1	77.4	1.3	3.09
Accelerated Supply/Conservation $8	98.2	75.8	16.9	2.34
Accelerated Supply/Conservation $13	96.0	72.8	5.0	2.82
Accelerated Supply/Conservation $16	96.4	73.1	1.3	2.84
Supply Pessimism $13	100.2	77.3	34.4	3.01
Supply Pessimism $16	98.7	75.6	31.6	3.24
Project Independence Report Scenarios				
Business as Usual $7	109.1	80.9	31.7	2.50
Business as Usual $11	102.9	76.1	7.1	2.91
Conservation $11	94.2	69.6	2.6	2.82
Accelerated Supply/Conservation $11	96.3	71.3	0	2.54
1975 Actual	71.0		13.2	3.24

Source: Author's estimates and unpublished data, Federal Energy Administration. Most of the data are summarized in Federal Energy Administration, *National Energy Outlook* (Washington, D.C.: U.S. Government Printing Office, 1976), Appendix G and Federal Energy Administration, *Project Independence Report* (Washington, D.C.: U.S. Government Printing Office, 1974). Appendix A1.

Note: Gross energy consumption includes inputs of energy into electrical generation. Net energy consumption only includes electricity distributed to other energy-consuming sectors. The difference between gross and net energy consumption reflects a production efficiency of approximately one-third in electrical generation. The average prices are based on net energy consumption. Prices for the *Project Independence Report* scenarios originally in 1973 dollars were restated in 1975 dollars using the consumer price index for those two years, per PIES conventions.

energy conservation, improved airline load factors, electric utility load management, and elimination of gas pilot lights. The Accelerated Supply scenarios assume aggressive, but achievable, efforts to increase domestic energy resource development, including accelerated leasing of outer continental shelf crude oil and natural gas rights, commercial development of naval petroleum reserves, expedited licensing of nuclear generating plants, and accelerated development of shale oil and synthetic fuels. The Accelerated Supply and Conservation scenarios combine the assumptions of the Conservation scenarios with those of the Accelerated Supply scenarios. The Supply Pessimism scenarios assume regional supply limitations, crude oil and natural gas ceilings of $9 per barrel and $1.20 per thousand cubic feet in 1975 dollars, unfavorable geologic finding rates and production levels, and reduced outer continental shelf leasing.

References

1. Executive Office of the President. *The National Energy Plan* (Washington, D.C.: U.S. Government Printing Office, 1977).

2. Federal Energy Administration. *National Energy Outlook* (Washington, D.C.: U.S. Government Printing Office, 1976).

3. Federal Energy Administration. *Project Independence Report* (Washington, D.C.: U.S. Government Printing Office, 1974).

4. Hall, Robert E. and Robert S. Pindyck. "The Conflicting Goals of National Energy Policy." *The Public Interest*, no. 47 (Spring 1977), pp. 3-15.

5. Mancke, Richard B. *The Failure of U.S. Energy Policy* (New York: Columbia University Press, 1974).

2

The Energy Crisis and the U.S. Economy, 1973–1975
David E. Serot

The Nature of the Crisis

In 1973-1974 the United States experienced an energy crisis involving two different shocks to the economy. One shock was the Arab oil embargo imposed against the United States and the Netherlands from October 1973 to March 1974. The embargo, although temporary, had psychological impacts on the economy. Producers, consumers, and government policy-makers became aware that the United States was threatened by its growing dependence on imported petroleum. This new awareness had the effect of focusing the attention of decision-makers in both the private and public sectors on the energy crisis to the neglect of the rest of the economy.[a]

The other shock was a quadrupling of world oil prices, which meant a permanent change in economic conditions and had serious repercussions on the U.S. economy. Sharply rising prices for imported petroleum led to increases in the prices of domestic petroleum and petroleum products, other forms of energy, and energy-intensive producer and consumer goods.

Table 2-1 shows the unit value index for imported petroleum and several wholesale price indexes (WPIs). The effects of increased world oil prices on domestic energy prices can be seen by the increase in the WPI for refined petroleum and the WPI for fuels and power. The effects of rising energy prices on the general price level are shown by the growth of the WPIs for food and fuel, industrial commodities, and all commodities. The energy-related increases in wholesale prices were passed on to consumers and added to inflationary pressures caused by the 1973 food price bulge.[b] Table 2-2 lists the consumer price indexes (CPIs) for several fuels and for all goods and services. It shows that the prices paid by consumers for gasoline, heating oil, natural gas, and electricity rose by 32 percent, 62 percent, 8 percent, and 13 percent, respectively, between 1973:1 and 1974:1.

The increases in world oil prices and the subsequent increases in other prices affected the U.S. economy in several ways. First, the higher world oil prices caused a transfer of wealth from U.S. consumers to foreign oil producers.

---

[a]The embargo did cause some unemployment, especially in the gasoline service station industry. For estimates of the effects of the embargo on employment, see [2]. Additional information on the causes and implications of the embargo can be found in [17] and [20].

[b]For a discussion of the 1973 rise in food prices, see [16].

7

Table 2-1
Unit Value Index for Imported Petroleum and Selected Wholesale Price Indexes

	Unit Value Index for Imported Petroleum (1972=100)	WPI for Refined Petroleum (1967=100)	WPI for Fuels and Power (1967=100)	WPI for Food and Feeds (1967=100)	WPI for Industrial Commodities (1967=100)	WPI (1967=100)
1973:1	106.4	117.3	126.0	142.4	121.3	126.9
1973:2	126.9	125.1	131.1	154.9	125.3	133.2
1973:3	131.6	130.5	135.2	184.5	126.7	142.1
1973:4	175.2	142.0	144.1	164.4	130.1	139.2
1974:1	379.7	186.8	177.4	180.6	138.2	149.5
1974:2	453.7	224.1	204.3	167.6	150.5	155.0
1974:3	472.6	242.1	226.0	183.4	161.6	167.4
1974:4	447.4	240.3	227.4	189.0	165.8	171.9
1975:1	457.3	241.8	232.3	179.5	168.4	171.3
1975:2	467.5	247.3	238.8	181.2	170.3	173.7
1975:3	447.8	266.5	252.4	189.0	172.2	176.7
1975:4	453.4	274.6	257.0	186.1	175.4	178.2

Source: Unpublished data, Bureau of Labor Statistics, U.S. Department of Labor.

Table 2-2
Selected Consumer Price Indexes

	Gasoline and Motor Oil (1967=100)	Heating Oil Fuel #2 (1967=100)	Gas, All Types (1967=100)	Electricity (1967=100)	Total (1967=100)
1973:1	112.4	125.1	126.6	122.6	128.7
1973:2	116.6	127.3	217.4	124.0	131.5
1973:3	119.2	132.0	126.7	125.0	134.4
1973:4	126.9	154.2	132.3	127.5	137.6
1974:1	148.1	202.1	136.9	137.7	141.4
1974:2	163.1	210.2	141.3	146.3	145.4
1974:3	165.3	219.1	146.0	150.8	149.9
1974:4	159.1	224.5	153.0	154.9	154.2
1975:1	160.1	224.4	162.4	163.0	157.0
1975:2	165.5	224.4	171.1	163.8	159.5
1975:3	177.2	231.3	173.4	169.2	162.9
1975:4	176.1	242.6	183.2	170.9	165.5

Source: Unpublished data, Bureau of Labor Statistics, U.S. Department of Labor.

Third, the general increase in prices reduced the real incomes of consumers and led to lower real personal consumption expenditures. Fourth, the unanticipated general increase in prices meant that planned investment expenditures purchased less real plant and equipment than expected.

Table 2-3 reveals the extent of the decline in economic activity that followed the increase in world petroleum prices. The reductions in real personal consumption expenditures and real investment brought about by rising energy prices contributed via the multiplier process to a serious decline in real GNP and higher unemployment. Real personal consumption expenditures began to fall in the second half of 1973 and were $15.9 billion below their 1973:3 level by 1975:1. Real investment declined steadily duing 1974 and then fell drastically in 1975:1. Real GNP declined by $12 billion, $10 billion, and $8 billion at annual rates in the first three quarters of 1974. It then declined by $20 billion in 1974:4 and by more than $30 billion in 1975:1. The unemployment rate rose as real GNP fell, peaking at 8.7 percent in 1975:2.

Despite the poor performance of the economy in 1974 and 1975, it would be incorrect to attribute the entire decline in economic activity to the energy crisis. As Table 2-3 shows, economic activity slowed down in early 1973 prior to the onset of the energy crisis. Both real personal consumption expenditures and real investment grew only marginally in the first three quarters of 1973. Real GNP increased by less than $7 billion during the same period, reflecting a virtual absence of economic growth. These data suggest that the energy crisis

Table 2-3
Real GNP, Investment, Consumption, and the Unemployment Rate
(Billions of 1972 Dollars)

	Real GNP	Real Investment				Real Personal Consumption				Unemployment Rate
		Total	Plant and Equipment	Change in Business Inventories	Residential Construction	Total	Durable Goods	Nondurable Goods	Services	
1973:1	1229.8	205.0	128.7	11.6	64.4	767.7	124.9	310.9	331.9	4.93
1973:2	1231.1	206.1	130.3	12.0	62.0	766.8	123.0	307.8	336.0	4.83
1973:3	1236.3	206.0	132.4	11.5	58.3	770.5	121.2	310.6	338.7	4.80
1973:4	1242.6	212.6	133.9	21.7	54.0	765.8	118.1	308.0	339.7	4.83
1974:1	1230.4	195.9	134.5	12.0	49.9	761.8	114.9	305.1	341.8	5.03
1974:2	1220.8	183.8	129.8	9.6	47.0	761.9	115.0	304.0	342.9	5.13
1974:3	1212.9	173.2	125.0	5.1	43.9	764.7	116.1	304.9	343.7	5.63
1974:4	1191.7	166.9	120.8	8.8	39.3	757.0	103.1	299.8	354.1	6.67
1975:1	1161.1	129.7	115.2	-21.5	35.4	754.6	106.0	300.6	348.0	8.13
1975:2	1177.1	124.1	110.9	-21.5	36.8	767.4	108.4	307.2	351.8	8.73
1975:3	1209.3	147.8	110.7	- 1.9	39.6	775.3	115.1	306.8	353.4	8.60
1975:4	1219.2	153.7	113.0	- 7.0	41.9	783.9	118.0	309.5	356.4	8.47

Source: Selected tables in U.S. Department of Commerce, Survey of Current Business 56, no. 7 (July 1976).

may have worsened the 1974-1975 recession without being the sole cause of it, even though the crisis was clearly the most visible factor involved in the downturn.

Simulation Studies of the Crisis

Several investigations have estimated the effects of the energy crisis on the U.S. economy with large-scale econometric forecasting models by comparing simulations of how the economy would have performed without the energy crisis with simulations of how the economy actually performed.[c] These studies indicate that even without the energy crisis the economy was heading into a recession in 1974-1975, but that the crisis exacerbated this recession and added to the loss in economic growth that otherwise would have occurred.

In the 1974 *Project Independence Report*, the FEA compared Embargo and No Embargo forecasts using both the Data Resources, Inc. (DRI) and Department of Commerce (DOC) models.[d] Table 2-4 summarizes the results of this study. DRI model forecasts made before and after the embargo were compared on the assumption that differences between them reflected only the effects of the embargo. A DOC model forecast made after the embargo and a modified version of it designed to eliminate the effects of the embargo were

Table 2-4
Project Independence Report Embargo Simulations with the DRI and DOC Models (Real GNP in Billions of 1972 Dollars)

	DRI		DOC	
	No Embargo	Embargo	No Embargo	Embargo
1973:4	1283.5	1277.8	1281.0	1277.8
1974:1	1283.7	1257.2	1274.5	1258.7
1974:2	1294.6	1265.1	1283.7	1269.0
1974:3	1304.9	1279.0	1294.7	1279.3
1974:4	1315.8	1294.4	1311.7	1289.7
1975:1	1331.2	1307.5	1324.2	1301.5

Source: Federal Energy Administration, *Project Independence Report* (Washington, D.C.: U.S. Government Printing Office, 1974), Table AV-7.
Note: Original data in 1958 dollars have been restated in 1972 dollars.

---

[c]For discussions of the use of large-scale econometric models in simulation, especially the limitations and problems of this methodology, see [9] and [11, pp. 235-38].

[d]The differences in the forecasts generated by the models reflect different structures of the models. See Appendix A-V in [4], especially p. A-219.

compared. Unfortunately, the study did not take completely into account the increase in world petroleum prices and was undertaken too soon after the embargo to permit the actual course of economic activity in 1974 and 1975 to be analyzed.

The study found that the embargo caused a reduction in real GNP during 1973:4 and 1974:1, followed by recovery through 1975:1, the last quarter considered. With both models, the 1975:1 level of real GNP in 1972 dollars in the Embargo simulation was about $23 billion below its level in the No Embargo simulation, most of the reduction coming in personal consumption expenditures. With both models, the level of investment in the Embargo simulation fell below its level in the No Embargo simulation for the first two quarters and then rose to approach its level in the No Embargo simulation by 1975:1. These results suggest that the embargo imposed a one-time transfer of income from U.S. consumers to foreign oil producers, thereby reducing personal consumption expenditures and delaying investment.

In late 1975 a second FEA study was undertaken by Stephen Chapel, who created four alternative simulations of the DRI model by modifying a historical simulation of that model.[e] Table 2–5 summarizes the results of this study. In Scenario I, the WPI for fuels and power and unit value indexes for imported crude oil and refined petroleum products were specified to grow at an 8 percent annual rate, and the real value of petroleum imports was adjusted with projections from an FEA petroleum demand forecasting model. In Scenario II, nominal government expenditures were reduced to keep real government expenditures consistent with historical simulation levels, since lower inflation rates in Scenario I increased government expenditures in real terms. In Scenario III, WPIs for textiles, wood products, and metal products which declined in Scenarios I and II were held constant. In Scenario IV, reserves for private nonbank deposits at commercial banks (RPDs) were reduced to maintain tight money, since the monetary policy of the historical simulation was equivalent to an expansionary monetary policy in Scenarios I, II, and III because of the lower inflation rate. The adjustment was made by reducing RPDs enough to keep the interest rate on three-month Treasury bills at historical levels.

As Tables 2-3 and 2-5 indicate, the historical simulation closely tracked the steady decline in real GNP during the first three quarters of 1974 and its sharp falling off in 1974:4 and 1975:1. All four alternative simulations show a milder recession occurring in late 1974 and early 1975 without the energy crisis. In Scenarios I through III, real GNP declined in 1973.4 and 1974:1, recovered in the next two quarters, and then fell sharply in 1974:4 and 1975:1. In Scenario IV, real GNP declined steadily throughout 1974 and 1975:1, reflecting the imposition of tighter monetary policy than in the other three alternative scenarios.

In the May 1976 *Report to Congress on the Economic Impact of Energy*

---

[e]See [1].

Table 2-5
Chapel Embargo Simulations with the DRI Model

	Historical Simulation	Scenario I	Scenario II	Scenario III	Scenario IV
	Real GNP in Billions of 1972 dollars				
1973:4	1281.4	1279.3	1278.8	1278.9	1281.0
1974:1	1259.0	1261.8	1260.9	1260.9	1262.5
1974:2	1253.1	1272.0	1267.5	1267.5	1262.7
1974:3	1246.2	1281.4	1276.4	1276.4	1260.9
1974:4	1217.6	1266.9	1259.8	1258.4	1236.2
1975:1	1179.2	1240.4	1232.6	1230.9	1192.9
1975:2	1177.8	1258.9	1250.4	1247.2	1199.4
	GNP Implicit Price Deflator				
1973:4	158.8	159.0	158.6	158.7	158.7
1974:1	163.4	163.1	162.8	162.8	162.8
1974:2	167.2	165.9	165.3	165.3	165.5
1974:3	171.9	168.6	168.1	168.1	168.3
1974:4	177.8	172.5	171.5	171.8	172.0
1975:1	181.4	174.5	173.4	174.2	174.6
1975:2	183.6	174.6	173.9	175.3	175.7
	Unemployment Rate				
1973:4	4.8	4.8	4.8	4.8	4.7
1974:1	5.1	5.1	5.1	5.1	5.1
1974:2	5.1	4.9	5.0	5.0	5.0
1974:3	5.5	5.0	5.1	5.1	5.2
1974:4	6.6	5.7	5.8	5.8	6.2
1975:1	8.4	7.0	7.2	7.2	7.9
1975:2	8.9	7.0	7.3	7.3	8.4

Source: Stephen W. Chapel, "The Impact of Higher Energy Prices on the U.S. Economy: 1973-1974," Technical Report 75-21, Office of Economic Impact Analysis, Federal Energy Administration, (November 1974).

Note: Original real GNP data in 1958 daollars have been restated in 1972 dollars. The GNP implicit price deflators reported here were computed by the author from data in the Chapel report; Chapel only reported percentage changes in the GNP implicit price deflator.

Actions, the FEA presented a third analysis of the energy crisis performed with three simulations of the DRI model.[f] Table 2-6 summarizes the results of this study. A DRI historical simulation was selected as the Base Case. It was modified to produce a counterfactual No Disruption simulation by specifying annual rises in world and domestic petroleum prices of 8 percent and 16 percent, respectively.[g]

[f]See [5].

[g]A number of other adjustments were also made to incorporate FEA estimates of what the economy would have looked like in the absence of the crisis. For details, see Appendix B in [5].

Table 2–6
Report to Congress **Embargo Simulations with the DRI Model**

	Base Case	No Disruption	No Disruption with Tight Money
	Real GNP in Billions of 1972 Dollars		
1973:4	1280.8	1266.0	1271.0
1974:1	1256.3	1258.3	1257.0
1974:2	1250.7	1265.4	1253.9
1974:3	1243.8	1268.0	1245.9
1974:4	1214.4	1253.4	1221.1
1975:1	1175.8	1237.1	1197.8
1975:2	1180.2	1257.1	1211.7
1975:3	1218.0	1307.5	1255.3
1975:4	1233.8	1335.0	1278.8
	GNP Implicit Price Deflator		
1973:4	159.1	158.8	N/A
1974:1	163.8	162.2	N/A
1974:2	167.5	165.2	N/A
1974:3	172.2	167.8	N/A
1974:4	178.2	171.9	N/A
1975:1	181.7	173.5	N/A
1975:2	183.9	173.9	N/A
1975:3	186.1	174.5	N/A
1975:4	189.2	176.4	N/A
	Unemployment Rate		
1973:4	4.7	4.9	4.8
1974:1	5.2	5.3	5.2
1974:2	5.2	5.1	5.2
1974:3	5.6	5.2	5.5
1974:4	6.7	5.9	6.6
1975:1	8.5	7.2	8.1
1975:2	9.1	7.3	8.4
1975:3	8.5	6.4	7.6
1975:4	8.6	6.1	7.4

Source: Federal Energy Administration, *Report to Congress on the Economic Impact of Energy Actions*, NTIS PB-256-684 (Springfield, Va.: National Technical Information Service, 1976).

Note: Original data in 1958 dollars have been restated in 1972 dollars.

In turn this simulation was modified to produce a No Disruption with Tight Money simulation by adjusting RPDs as Chapel did in his Scenario IV simulation. This study found that a recession would have occurred without the energy crisis, whether monetary policy were tight or loose, and that it was made worse by the crisis and tight money.

A non-FEA study of the energy crisis by George L. Perry was published in *Higher Oil Prices and the World Economy*.[h] Perry simulated both the Federal Reserve Board (FRB) and University of Michigan models for Energy Crisis and No Energy Crisis scenarios. Table 2-7 summarizes his results. Perry found that real GNP in 1972 dollars was $38 billion to $57 billion lower by the end of 1975 with the crisis than it would have been without the crisis. This impact is comparable with those reported in the FEA studies. However, Perry did not report levels of real GNP, so the behavior of the economy over time implied by his simulations cannot be uniquely characterized. If his Energy Crisis simulations yielded unemployment consistent with the actual ones of 8 percent and more for 1975, then his No Energy Crisis simulations would have yielded unemployment rates between 6 percent and 7 percent for 1975. Such unemployment rates imply a recession in 1974-1975 without the energy crisis. If his Energy Crisis simulations yielded unemployment rates of 6 percent for 1975, then his No Energy Crisis simulations would have yielded unemployment rates between 4 percent and 5 percent for 1975, indicating a very mild downturn at worst.

Economic Activity in the Private Sector

Economic interactions during the 1973-1975 period were complex. Close examination of the data in Table 2-3 on real personal consumption expenditures and real investment indicates that the energy crisis contributed to the length and severity of the 1974-1975 recession, but was not the fundamental cause of it. The economy showed definite signs of a slowdown in 1973, prior to the energy crisis. Consumer demand for durable and nondurable goods was off; investment in plant and equipment was weak; inventories were accumulating; housing construction was declining.

Real personal consumption expenditures for durable goods in 1972 dollars declined steadily during 1973, then fell sharply in 1974:1. They increased slowly over the next two quarters, but fell by $13 billion in 1974:4. Real personal consumption expenditures for nondurable goods in 1972 dollars fluctuated during 1973, then declined by almost $3 billion in 1974:1. After remaining virtually unchanged for the next two quarters, they fell by just over $5 billion in 1974:4. They spurted back up in 1975:2 and then grew slowly during the rest of that year. Real personal consumption expenditures for services in 1972

---

[h]See [12].

Table 2-7
Perry Embargo Simulations with the FRB and University of Michigan Models

	FRB	Michigan
Real GNP Differences in Billions of 1972 Dollars		
1973:4	− 5.2	− 3.7
1974:1	−15.1	− 8.6
1974:2	−22.7	−14.3
1974:3	−28.0	−20.3
1974:4	−33.6	−31.4
1975:1	−35.0	−37.1
1975:2	−35.9	−44.6
1975:3	−37.1	−51.4
1975:4	−37.8	−56.8
GNP Implicit Price Deflator Percent Differences		
1973:4	0.1	0.2
1974:1	1.0	1.0
1974:2	1.1	1.5
1974:3	1.4	1.9
1974:4	1.5	2.6
1975:1	1.7	3.3
1975:2	1.9	3.9
1975:3	2.2	4.4
1975:4	2.4	4.8
Unemployment Rate Percentage Point Differences		
1973:4	0.1	0.1
1974:1	0.4	0.2
1974:2	0.8	0.3
1974:3	1.0	0.5
1974:4	1.1	0.8
1975:1	1.2	1.0
1975:2	1.3	1.3
1975:3	1.4	1.6
1975:4	1.6	1.7

Source: Adapted from George L. Perry, "The United States," in Fried and Schultze, eds., *Higher Oil Prices and the World Economy* (Washington, D.C.: The Brookings Institution, 1975), p. 96–7.

Note: Differences are for Energy Crisis simulations relative to No Energy Crisis simulations. Original data in 1973 dollars have been restated in 1972 dollars.

dollars grew steadily throughout 1974, fell by a little more than $6 billion in 1975:1, and then resumed increasing.

Real investment in plant and equipment in 1972 dollars grew at about 4 percent per year through 1974:1, declined steadily by $4 billion to $5 billion each quarter until 1975:2, and then turned up in the last half of 1975. Inventories in 1972 dollars rose ominously during 1973, peaking at a $24.4 billion increase in 1973:4. They accumulated more slowly during 1974 and then fell drastically at a $20 billion rate in the first half of 1975. Investment in nonfarm housing in 1972 dollars fell steadily from its 1973:1 level until 1975:2, when it had declined by almost 50 percent.

The onset of the energy crisis in 1973:4 had variable effects on different parts of the economy. On the one hand, real personal consumption expenditures for nondurable goods declined rapidly in 1973:4 and 1974:1, reflecting reduced use of gasoline and fuel oil as a result of their unavailability and higher prices.[i] On the other hand, personal consumption expenditures for durable goods declined more as the result of higher new car prices than as a result of the energy crisis. Automobile sales peaked in early 1973 and started to decline in 1973:2. Increased new car prices for the 1974 model year were announced prior to the embargo and led to a continuation of this decline. The end of the 1972-1973 automobile sales boom had been anticipated for some time, although it was undeniably compounded by the adverse psychological climate that the embargo and long lines at gasoline stations created.[j] Between 1973:3 and 1974:4 real personal consumption expenditures for autos and parts in 1972 dollars declined by $4 billion compared to a decline of $3.2 billion in real personal consumption expenditures for all durable goods.[k]

Higher energy and other prices began seriously to affect real personal consumption expenditures in 1974. The energy-related inflation both reduced real personal income and drove tax collections up. Together these impacts drove real disposable income in 1972 dollars down by $20 billion in the first three quarters of the year. This erosion of purchasing power, together with large increases in new car prices for the 1975 model year after "extraordinary" increases in them for the 1974 model year, caused automobile sales to drop at an annual rate of 3.0 million units in 1974:4.[l]

Higher energy and other prices, along with higher interest rates they engendered, also began seriously to affect real investment in 1974. Unanticipated

---

[i]Real personal consumption expenditures for gasoline, motor oil, and fuel oil fell by $3.2 billion in 1974:1, which exceeded the $2.9 billion decline in real personal consumption expenditures for all nondurable goods. See Table 2.4 in [19].

[j]See [14, pp. 42–43].

[k]See Table 2.4 in [19].

[l]See [14, pp. 41–44] and [15, p. 66].

inflation related to higher energy prices rendered obsolete capital budgets for major investment projects involving long lead times, causing significant shortfalls in actual purchases of plant and equipment.[m] The strain on capital budgets was exacerbated by tight monetary policy, aimed at slowing the inflation, that pushed interest rates to record levels by 1974:3. The spurt in interest rates also hurt the housing industry, which had been in a slump since the start of 1973, making inevitable the plunge in home-building and the purchase of mobile homes in the second half of 1973.[n] Rising energy prices should have induced investment in the energy sector, but increases in the oil industry merely offset previously planned retrenchments in mining and electric utilities.[o] Thus, total investment in the energy sector did not rise to offset declines in other sectors.

Finally, in 1974:4 stagnant real consumption expenditures and declining real fixed investment led to a precipitous swing from inventory accumulation to decumulation. Businessmen who had attributed the weak state of the economy to the temporary effects of the energy crisis realized that ". . . they were holding up the economy merely by selling goods to one another and retaining workers they did not need." Inventories in 1972 dollars fell by $21 billion in both 1974:4 and 1975:1, as ". . . . a trimming of personnel and production that might have been accomplished gradually earlier in the year took place abruptly and frenetically. . . ."[p] As a result, real GNP in 1972 dollars fell by approximately $21 billion in 1974:4 and by more than $30 billion in 1975:1.

Fiscal and Monetary Policy

Government tax and spending policies played a definite role in exacerbating the 1974-1975 recession. The federal government ran a full employment budget surplus each quarter between 1973:3 and 1975:1, averaging almost $28 billion during the last three quarters of 1974.[q] State and local tax receipts rose with inflation during this period, but grew little in real terms. Faced with rising

---

[m]The implicit price deflator index (1972=100) for producers' fixed investment rose from 106 in 1973:4 to 125 by 1974:4. Nominal nonresidential fixed investment increased from $140.3 billion in 1973:4 to $151.9 billion in 1974:4, but real investment in plant and equipment in 1972 dollars fell from $132.4 billion to $121.8 billion over the same period. See [10, p. 214], Table A-4 in [18], and Table 1.2 in] 19].

[n]See [10, p. 213].

[o]See [12, pp. 92-93].

[p]See [10, p. 214].

[q]The full employment surplus is a measure of the budget surplus or deficit that would occur, given tax rates and levels of discretionary expenditures, if the economy were at full employment. See [3, pp. 241-42].

demands for unemployment compensation and welfare, state and local governments were forced to raise taxes or reduce other expenditures.

Fiscal policy was not deliberately restrictive following the energy crisis. It simply turned out that way as the result of shortfalls in most major categories of federal expenditures and an underestimate of the effects that inflation would have on tax collections. A large deficit in the federal budget was expected for 1974, because of the operation of automatic stabilizers during the downturn. However, the automatic stabilizers proved ineffective as a result of the inflation induced by rising energy prices. Personal taxes rose as a percentage of personal income despite the recession, reducing the amount of money that consumers had to spend and curbing aggregate demand.[r]

Effective countercyclical action was not taken by the government until March 1975, when Congress passed a $21 billion tax reduction program. This package contained a 12 percent rebate on 1974 personal income taxes, up to a maximum rebate of $1,000, and a $4 billion investment tax credit requested by President Ford. The tax package reversed the 1974 rise in personal tax rates, produced a full employment deficit of more than $33 billion in the federal budget during 1975:2, and helped spur a recovery in the economy that was only temporarily slowed by a jump in tax collections during 1975:3.[s]

As did government tax and spending policies, monetary policy in 1974 made the 1974–1975 downturn worse. The main difference was that the Federal Reserve intentionally pursued a restrictive course. Throughout the first three quarters of 1974, the Federal Open Market Committee concentrated on combating inflation by limiting the growth of the money supply.[t] As a consequence of this conscious policy, the annual rate of change in M_1 declined from 7.6 percent in 1973:1 to 4.3 percent in 1974:3. By 1974:3 money had become tight enough to force interest rates to record levels. The federal funds rate went above 13 percent in July and averaged 12 percent for the quarter as a whole. Other short-term interest rates reached comparable levels, driving investment down as already discussed.

When economic activity declined sharply in late 1974, at least partly because of the credit crunch of 1974:3, the Federal Open Market Committee attempted to reverse its course and ease monetary conditions. The open market account manager was directed to expand the money supply by 6 percent to 8 percent in 1974:4 and 1975:1, but he was not able to bring its growth under control until later in 1975. Notwithstanding his efforts, M_1 grew at annual rates of 4.2

---

[r]The shortfall in government expenditures occurred both in real and nominal terms. For discussions of the points made in this paragraph, see [14, pp. 60-64] and [15, p. 59].

[s]See [15, pp. 48, 55].

[t]Minutes of the Federal Open Market Committee meetings are published approximately sixty to ninety days after each meeting in the *Federal Reserve Bulletin* published by the Federal Reserve System.

percent in 1974:4 and only 0.5 percent in 1975:1 as falling economic activity reduced the demand for money.[u]

Summary and Conclusions

The 1973-1974 energy crisis came at a particularly bad time for the United States economy. Real personal consumption expenditures and real nonresidential fixed investment had begun to stagnate; residential construction was sliding into a deep decline; and inventories were increasing at a dangerous rate prior to the crisis. Moreover, the fiscal and monetary authorities failed to take appropriate action once the crisis hit. Because they underestimated the effects of inflation on tax revenues and overestimated government spending in both real and nominal terms, the fiscal authorities allowed the public sector to act as a drag on the economy at precisely the wrong time. Similarly, the Federal Reserve was so preoccupied with curbing inflation that it failed to perceive the downturn and pursued a tight money policy. Designed to reduce inflation at the cost of a modest rise in unemployment, tight money actually contributed to a major recession with employment approaching 9 percent.[v]

The energy crisis made the economic situation worse in at least three ways. First, the fourfold rise in world oil prices caused inflationary pressures that reduced real income, real personal consumption expenditures, and real investment. Second, the embargo created a psychological climate of uncertainty that further retarded aggregate demand, especially that for automobiles when coupled with the higher new car prices for the 1974 and 1975 model years. Third, the crisis played a major role in misleading policy-makers by focusing their attention away from the underlying weakness of the economy.[w]

Did the energy crisis cause the 1974-1975 recession? On the one hand, the evidence indicates definitely not, since the economy would have slumped without the crisis. On the other hand, there can be no doubt that the decline would have been significantly less severe if the energy crisis had not occurred.

---

[u]For a discussion of monetary policy during 1974 and the Federal Reserve's difficulties in trying to increase the money supply in late 1974, see [13].

[v]See [8, p. 141], [11], and [13, pp. 125-26].

[w]In January 1974 one member of the Federal Open Market Committee opposed any easing of monetary restraint, because ". . . the actual and prospective slowdown in economic activity resulted from capacity, supply and price-distorting controls rather than from a weakening in demand. . . ." In September 1974, a member of the same committee opposed a decision to ease the growth of the money supply, because he thought that ". . . inflation and inflationary expectations continued unabated whereas the probabilities were against the development of a severe recession." See [6, p. 281] and [7, p. 847].

References

1. Chapel, Stephen W. "The Impact of Higher Energy Prices on the U.S. Economy: 1973-1974." Technical Report 75-21, Office of Economic Impact Analysis, Federal Energy Administration (November 1974).

2. Early, John F. "Effects of the Energy Crisis on Employment." *Monthly Labor Review* (August 1974), pp. 8-16.

3. Eckaus, Richard S. *Basic Economics* (Boston: Little, Brown and Company, 1972).

4. Federal Energy Administration. *Project Independence Report* (Washington, D.C.: Government Printing Office, 1974).

5. Federal Energy Administration. *Report to Congress on the Economic Impact of Energy Actions*, NTIS PB-256-684 (Springfield, Va.' National Technical Information Service, 1976).

6. Federal Reserve System. "Record of Policy Actions of the Federal Open Market Committee." *Federal Reserve Bulletin* 60, no. 4 (April 1974), pp. 275-83.

7. Federal Reserve System. "Record of Policy Actions of the Federal Open Market Committee." *Federal Reserve Bulletin* 60, no. 12 (December 1974), pp. 842-48.

8. Modigliani, Franco and Lucas Papademos. "Targets for Monetary Policy in the Coming Year." *Brookings Papers on Economic Activity*, no. 1 (1975), pp. 141-63.

9. Naylor, Thomas H. "Policy Simulation Experiments with Macroeconomics Models: The State of the Art." *Journal of Agricultural Economics* 52, no. 2 (May 1970), pp. 263-71.

10. Okun, Arthur M. "A Postmortem of the 1974 Recession." *Brookings Papers on Economic Activity*, no. 1 (1975), pp. 207-21.

11. Perry, George L. "Policy Alternatives for 1974." *Brookings Papers on Economic Activity*, no. 1 (1975), pp. 222-37.

12. Perry, George L. "The United States." In Fried and Schultze, eds., *Higher Oil Prices and the World Economy* (Washington, D.C.: The Brookings Institution, 1975), pp. 71-104.

13. Poole, William. "Monetary Policy During the Recession." *Brookings Papers on Economic Activity*, no. 1 (1975), pp. 123-40.

14. *Report of the Council of Economic Advisors* (Washington, D.C.: U.S. Government Printing Office, 1975).

15. *Report of the Council of Economic Advisors* (Washington, D.C.: U.S. Government Printing Office, 1976).

16. Schnittker, John A. "The 1972-1973 Food Price Spiral." *Brookings Papers on Economic Activity*, no. 2 (1973), pp. 498-506.

17. Sobel, L.A., ed. *Israel and the Arabs: The October 1973 War* (New York: Facts on File, Inc., 1974).

18. U.S. Department of Commerce. *Business Conditions Digest* (August 1974).

19. U.S. Department of Commerce. *Survey of Current Business* 56, no. 7 (July 1976).

20. Yager, Joseph A. and Eleanor B. Steinberg. "Trends in the International Oil Market." In Fried and Schultze, eds., *Higher Oil Prices and the World Economy* (Washington, D.C.: The Brookings Institution, 1975), pp. 227-75.

3

Changing Energy Consumption Patterns in U.S. Manufacturing
William G. Rice and Eugene Rossidivito

The pattern of energy consumption in the manufacturing sector has changed substantially during the past decade as the result of a rise in the relative price of energy, the emergence of new technologies, the imposition of environmental constraints, and other factors. Though it would be convenient to associate most of the change with the 1973–1974 Arab oil embargo and the quadrupling of oil prices by OPEC, energy consumption patterns in the manufacturing sector began changing well before 1973. However, the energy crisis did usher in a new era of energy awareness and accelerate changes already under way.

This chapter examines the way energy consumption patterns in manufacturing as a whole and the thirteen largest energy consuming industries in manufacturing changed during the period from 1967 to 1974. The analysis is presented in three sections. The first section describes the data used. The second section discusses the energy consumption pattern changes that occurred in manufacturing as a whole and in the thirteen individual industries. The final section considers some economic reasons for the energy consumption pattern changes.

The Data

This chapter uses data gathered by the Bureau of the Census for the years 1967, 1971, and 1974. The 1967 and 1971 data come from the *Fuels and Electric Energy Consumed* supplements to the *1967 Census of Manufacturers* and the *1972 Census of Manufacturers*, respectively; the 1974 data come from a supplement to the *1974 Annual Survey of Manufacturers*.[a] Accordingly, the data conform to Census definitions and cover only purchased fuels and electric energy used "as purchased" to generate heat and power. The data provide physical quantity and total cost information for distillate fuel oil, residual fuel oil, coal, coke, natural gas, and purchased electricity, as well as total cost information for other fuels and fuels not specified by kind (NSK).[b] The data

---

[a]See [2], [3], and [4].

[b]The physical quantities of energy consumed were converted to kilowatt-hour equivalents (KHEs) for comparative purposes as follows: distillate oil 1,707 KHEs per barrel; residual oil 1,842 KHEs per barrel; coal 7,677 KHEs per short ton; natural gas 303.3 KHEs per million cubic feet; coke 7,618 KHEs per short ton; and other fuels at 168.6 KHEs per dollar. Other fuels include purchased steam, wood, gasoline, liquid petroleum gases, mixed gases, coke-oven gases, still gases, blast furnace gases, and small amounts of miscellaneous fuels.

23

do not cover feedstocks—that is, energy products consumed in the manufacturing process—or captive energy.

The data suffer from several limitations. Omitting the consumption of feedstocks and captive energy understates total requirements for energy resources. This problem is particularly serious for petroleum refining, Standard Industrial Classification (SIC) industry 2911, and blast furnaces and steel mills, SIC industry 3312, where captive sources often provide more energy than is purchased.[c] As another example, bark, hogged fuel, spent liquors, and other waste products are estimated to account for almost half of current energy consumption in the pulp and paper industry.

The Bureau of the Census is required by law to aggregate and otherwise disguise the data it publishes to avoid identifying individual firms. This confidentiality requirement results in incomplete consumption reports for specific fuels in certain industries, biasing apparent energy consumption downward in these industries and reducing the reliability of industry fuel comparisons.[d]

Energy consumption is an incomplete measure by itself, because it does not reflect how efficiently energy is used. Federal Reserve Board Indexes of Industrial Production (FRB Indexes) are used as a measure of physical output to provide such a perspective. Total energy consumption measured in billions of kilowatt-hour equivalents (KHEs) is divided by the appropriate FRB Index to give a measure of energy efficiency which can be compared over time for manufacturing as a whole and for each of the thirteen individual industries.[e] Reductions in the ratio of consumption to output over time indicate increasing energy efficiency.

Energy Consumption Pattern Changes

Manufacturing as a Whole

Total Consumption. Table 3-1 reports the total KHE and fuel-specific physical quantities of purchased energy consumed in manufacturing as a whole and the thirteen individual industries during 1967, 1971, and 1974. Table 3-2 reports the corresponding average dollar costs per 1000 KHEs. Table 3-1 shows that

---

[c]See [1, p. 15].

[d]In some instances small establishments report the total cost of fuels, but do not report the costs and quantities of specific fuels.

[e]Energy efficiency is not synonymous with economic efficiency or profit maximization. Prior to the escalation of energy prices, "in many industries capital and energy were freely substituted for labor, lowering total costs and increasing profits, but at the same time raising the energy-output ratio." Once energy prices had risen, such substitution often became inefficient. See [1, p. 10].

consumption of purchased energy in manufacturing as a whole increased by 11 percent from 3.46 trillion KHEs in 1967 to 3.85 trillion KHEs in 1971 and then by another 2 percent to 3.92 trillion KHEs in 1974. Table 3-2 shows that the $4.96 per 1000 KHEs average cost of total purchased energy consumption in 1974 exceeded the $2.71 per 1000 KHEs average cost in 1971 by 83 percent, whereas the latter was only 22 percent higher than the $2.22 per 1000 KHEs average cost in 1967.

Although total purchased energy consumption and its cost rose by about the same extent between 1967 and 1971, the cost increased much more rapidly between 1971 and 1974 as a result of the price increases that accompanied the 1973-1974 Arab oil embargo. The total cost of purchased energy rose by 13 percent from $7.8 billion in 1967 to $10.4 billion in 1971 and then by another 87 percent to $19.5 billion in 1974.

Table 3-3 reports the energy efficiency ratios described above for manufacturing as a whole and the thirteen individual industries in 1967, 1971, and 1974. These efficiency ratios strongly imply that higher energy prices encouraged manufacturers to use purchased energy more efficiently. Energy efficiency declined by 1.4 percent per year between 1967 and 1971 when energy prices were relatively stable, but then rose by 4.8 percent per year between 1971 and 1974 when energy prices climbed rapidly. Many of the improvements in energy efficiency between 1971 and 1974 were undoubtedly one-time improvements attributable to belt tightening and housekeeping measures. Such efficiency gains cannot be expected to continue indefinitely without substantial capital investment.

Specific Fuels. As Table 3-1 shows, interfuel substitution significantly affected the fuel mix of total purchased energy consumption in manufacturing as a whole during the 1967-1974 period. The most striking shifts were steady increases in the shares of fuel oil and electricity usage, a steady decrease in the share of coal usage, and a peaking in the share of natural gas usage.

Distillate and residual oil usage increased from 9 percent of total purchased energy consumption in 1967 to 11 percent in 1971 and 13 percent in 1974. Consumption of these two fuels grew by 59 percent and 25 percent, respectively, between 1967 and 1971, but only by 18 percent and 14 percent, respectively, between 1971 and 1974 when their prices began to rise sharply. While the average dollar cost of distillate oil rose by only 19 percent from $2.12 per 1000 KHEs in 1967 to $2.53 per 1000 KHEs in 1971, it jumped by 172 percent to $6.88 per 1000 KHEs in 1974. Similarly, while the average dollar cost of residual oil rose by 45 percent from $1.43 per 1000 KHEs in 1967 to $2.07 per 1000 KHEs in 1971, it jumped by 203 percent to $6.28 per 1000 KHEs in 1974.

Electricity grew from 12 percent of total purchased energy consumption in 1967 to 13 percent in 1971 and 16 percent in 1974. Its average dollar cost rose by 14 percent from $8.69 per 1000 KHEs in 1967 to $9.87 per 1000 KHEs

Table 3-1

Purchased Energy Consumption in 1967, 1971, and 1974 (Fuel Shares in Parentheses)

	Total (Billion KHEs)			Distillate Oil (1000 Barrels)			Residual Oil (1000 Barrels)			Coal (1000 Short Tons)		
	1967	1971	1974	1967	1971	1974	1967	1971	1974	1967	1971	1974
All Manufacturers	3,461 (100.0)	3,847 (100.0)	3,925 (100.0)	65,654 (3.2)	104,949 (4.7)	124,357 (5.4)	112,959 (6.0)	140,726 (6.7)	160,765 (7.5)	75,100 (16.7)	61,393 (12.3)	47,790 (9.3)
2911 Petroleum Refining	386 (100.0)	445 (100.0)	435 (100.0)	354 (0.2)	1,574 (0.6)	D	6,909 (3.3)	9,842 (4.1)	5,732 (2.4)	777 (1.5)	345 (0.6)	303 (0.5)
3312 Blast Furnaces and Steel Mills	416 (100.0)	408 (100.0)	448 (100.0)	11,960 (4.9)	11,354 (4.7)	11,345 (4.4)	18,934 (8.4)	16,426 (7.4)	32,507 (13.4)	5,719 (10.6)	5,085 (9.6)	3,476 (6.0)
2869 Industrial Organic Chemicals, N.E.C.	232 (100.0)	251 (100.0)	289 (100.0)	1,168 (0.9)	2,254 (1.5)	2,770 (1.6)	1,575 (1.2)	2,104 (1.5)	5,790 (3.7)	5,546 (18.3)	5,037 (15.4)	3,070 (8.2)
2621 Papermills, Except Building Paper	149 (100.0)	171 (100.0)	168 (100.0)	3,464 (4.0)	7,451 (7.4)	10,628 (10.8)	13,156 (16.3)	19,455 (20.9)	19,011 (20.9)	7,458 (38.5)	5,679 (25.5)	5,255 (24.0)
2631 Paperboard Mills	126 (100.0)	135 (100.0)	150 (100.0)	5,140 (7.0)	6,989 (8.9)	10,833 (12.4)	11,552 (16.9)	19,247 (26.3)	23,063 (28.4)	4,880 (29.8)	3,124 (17.8)	2,653 (13.6)
3241 Cement, Hydraulic	137 (100.0)	134 (100.0)	145 (100.0)	674 (0.8)	2,177 (2.8)	2,981 (3.5)	1,937 (2.6)	4,632 (6.3)	4,011 (5.1)	8,554 (48.1)	6,876 (39.3)	6,958 (36.9)
3334 Primary Aluminum	86 (100.0)	85 (100.0)	111 (100.0)	36	156 (0.3)	207 (0.3)	107 (0.2)	11	D	565 (5.0)	603 (5.5)	D
2812 Alkalies and Chlorine	54 (100.0)	50 (100.0)	53 (100.0)	192 (0.6)	291 (1.0)	513 (1.7)	436 (1.5)	406 (1.5)	D	2,992 (42.2)	3,049 (46.8)	2,377 (34.4)
2824 Synthetic Organic Fibers, Except Cellulosic	46 (100.0)	43 (100.0)	45 (100.0)	330 (2.2)	1,729 (6.8)	2,400 (9.1)	426 (3.1)	2,689 (11.4)	5,410 (22.1)	1,785 (53.3)	2,297 (40.6)	2,077 (34.6)
2865 Cyclic Intermediates and Crudes	N/A (100.0)	40 (100.0)	41 (100.0)	N/A	3,149 (13.3)	3,106 (12.9)	N/A	1,599 (7.3)	2,478 (11.0)	N/A	497 (9.5)	468 (8.7)
3221 Glass Containers	35 (100.0)	42 (100.0)	41 (100.0)	281 (1.4)	1,048 (4.3)	1,603 (6.6)	1,156 (6.2)	431 (1.9)	1,660 (7.4)	S	–	–
3714 Motor Vehicle Parts and Accessories	31 (100.0)	37 (100.0)	36 (100.0)	217 (1.2)	820 (3.8)	704 (3.4)	613 (3.6)	518 (2.6)	486 (2.5)	1,285 (31.8)	1,104 (23.2)	824 (17.7)
3711 Motor Vehicles and Passenger Car Bodies	35 (100.0)	33 (100.0)	32 (100.0)	169 (0.8)	790 (4.1)	564 (3.0)	1,237 (6.6)	762 (4.3)	1,195 (6.8)	1,513 (33.5)	1,060 (24.7)	753 (17.9)

Table 3-1. Continued.

	Electricity (Millions KHEs)			Natural Gas (Billion Cu. Ft.)			Coke and Breeze (1000 Short Tons)			Other Fuels (Million Dollars)		
	1967	1971	1974	1967	1971	1974	1967	1971	1974	1967	1971	1974
All Manufacturers	427,465 (12.3)	514,613 (13.4)	616,803 (15.7)	5,307 (46.5)	6,454 (50.9)	6,340 (48.9)	13,562 (3.0)	13,743 (2.7)	14,690 (2.9)	220 (1.1)	377 (1.7)	710 (3.1)
2911 Petroleum Refining	17,474 (4.5)	22,524 (5.1)	25,824 (5.9)	1,101 (86.4)	1,291 (88.0)	1,138 (79.3)	–	–	D	8 (0.4)	29 (1.1)	D
3312 Blast Furnaces and Steel Mills	34,795 (8.4)	40,259 (9.9)	49,598 (11.1)	723 (52.7)	633 (47.0)	597 (40.4)	11,017 (20.2)	10,240 (19.1)	11,646 (20.0)	19 (0.8)	41 (1.7)	93 (3.5)
2869 Industrial Organic Chemicals, N.E.C.	13,378 (5.7)	19,701 (7.9)	18,391 (6.4)	522 (68.1)	586 (70.9)	702 (73.8)	–	D	3	21 (1.5)	36 (2.4)	43 (2.5)
2621 Papermills, Except Building Paper	12,777 (8.6)	16,955 (10.0)	18,496 (11.1)	132 (27.0)	195 (34.6)	164 (29.7)	–	–	–	7 (0.8)	7 (0.7)	19 (1.9)
2631 Paperboard Mills	5,294 (4.2)	6,740 (5.0)	9,847 (6.6)	144 (34.8)	175 (39.5)	169 (34.2)	–	–	–	8 (1.1)	9 (1.2)	19 (2.1)
3241 Cement, Hydraulic	7,495 (5.5)	8,515 (6.3)	9,905 (6.8)	183 (40.6)	202 (45.5)	199 (41.7)	–	S	D	–	S	1 (0.2)
3334 Primary Aluminum	41,957 (48.6)	42,712 (50.5)	68,699 (61.9)	131 (46.0)	121 (43.3)	D	–	–	D	–	D	2 (0.3)
2812 Alkalies and Chlorine	9,298 (17.1)	9,143 (18.3)	12,486 (23.6)	44 (24.7)	45 (27.4)	52 (29.9)	–	107 (1.6)	–	7 (2.1)	9 (3.2)	D
2824 Synthetic Organic Fibers, Except Cellulosic	2,539 (9.9)	4,843 (11.2)	6,840 (15.2)	26 (30.5)	41 (28.6)	27 (18.5)	–	–	–	1 (0.7)	–	1 (0.4)
2865 Cyclic Intermediates and Crudes	N/A	3,324 (8.2)	4,269 (10.4)	N/A	69 (52.2)	66 (48.7)	N/A	–	–	N/A	6 (2.6)	5 (2.1)
3221 Glass Containers	2,330 (6.7)	3,398 (8.2)	3,896 (9.5)	95 (82.9)	116 (84.7)	99 (73.2)	–	–	–	1 (0.4)	1 (0.4)	3 (1.2)
3714 Motor Vehicle Parts and Accessories	5,714 (21.7)	8,806 (24.1)	9,264 (25.9)	37 (31.0)	46 (37.9)	48 (40.3)	57 (1.4)	D	50 (1.1)	4 (2.1)	3 (1.4)	13 (6.2)
3711 Motor Vehicles and Passenger Car Bodies	6,734 (16.4)	6,676 (20.2)	6,155 (19.0)	32 (33.3)	45 (41.3)	47 (44.0)	–	–	52 (1.2)	S	9 (4.7)	14 (7.3)

Sources: U.S. Department of Commerce, Bureau of the Census, Annual Survey of Manufacturers 1974: Fuels and Electric Energy Consumed (Washington, D.C.: U.S. Government Printing Office, 1976). U.S. Department of Commerce, Bureau of the Census, 1972 Census of Manufacturers: Fuels and Electric Energy Consumed (Washington, D.C.: U.S. Government Printing Office, 1973). U.S. Department of Commerce, Bureau of the Census, 1967 Census of Manufacturers: Fuels and Electric Energy Consumed (Washington, D.C.: U.S. Government Printing Office, 1971).

Notes: Total includes estimates of those fuels not specified by kind (NSK). N/A = not available; D = data withheld to avoid identification of individual firms; S = data withheld because estimates do not meet Census Bureau standards for publication; – = zero.

Table 3–2

Purchased Energy Average Dollar Cost per 1000 Kilowatt-Hour Equivalents in 1967, 1971, and 1974

	Total KHE			Distillate			Residual			Coal		
	1967	1971	1974	1967	1971	1974	1967	1971	1974	1967	1971	1974
All Manufacturers	2.22	2.71	4.96	2.12	2.53	6.88	1.43	2.07	6.28	0.96	1.40	2.95
2911 Petroleum Refining	1.08	1.32	2.65	1.32	1.75	D	1.10	1.83	6.32	0.72	1.21	2.84
3312 Blast Furnaces and Steel Mills	2.11	2.82	5.45	1.89	2.55	7.50	1.77	2.23	6.95	0.90	1.23	3.17
2869 Industrial Organic Chemicals, N.E.C.	1.13	1.60	2.98	1.76	3.78	6.68	1.24	2.06	6.47	0.80	1.24	2.85
2621 Papermills, Except Building, Paper	1.67	2.19	4.78	1.42	1.97	6.11	1.27	1.94	5.63	1.06	1.45	3.09
2631 Paperboard Mills	1.37	1.91	4.54	1.37	2.15	6.22	1.18	1.78	5.56	1.01	1.52	3.35
3241 Cement, Hydraulic	1.39	1.81	3.40	2.17	2.13	6.27	1.35	1.68	5.17	0.93	1.40	2.64
3334 Primary Aluminum	2.05	2.56	4.14	3.24	2.63	6.52	1.53	5.12	D	1.29	1.34	D
2812 Alkalies and Chlorine	1.76	2.23	4.38	2.44	2.21	6.63	1.24	1.61	D	0.81	1.27	2.60
2824 Synthetic Organic Fibers, Except Cellulosic	1.61	2.21	5.47	2.31	2.10	7.32	1.40	1.86	5.98	0.96	1.47	3.14
2865 Cyclic Intermediates and Crudes	N/A	2.27	4.50	N/A	2.60	6.73	N/A	2.38	6.46	N/A	1.44	2.84
3221 Glass Containers	1.92	2.35	4.39	2.50	2.68	6.94	1.41	2.52	6.77	N/A	–	
3714 Motor Vehicle Parts and Accessories	3.54	4.35	7.28	2.43	2.57	7.32	1.77	2.20	6.26	1.04	1.76	3.46
3711 Motor Vehicles and Passenger Car Bodies	3.03	4.04	6.68	2.42	2.74	7.68	1.32	2.14	6.45	1.12	1.72	3.56

Table 3-2. Continued.

	Electricity			Natural Gas			Coke and Breeze		
	1967	1971	1974	1967	1971	1974	1967	1971	1976
All Manufacturers	8.69	9.87	13.80	1.09	1.31	2.25	2.41	3.03	6.67
2911 Petroleum Refining	7.03	7.69	11.73	0.76	0.87	1.80	–	–	D
3312 Blast Furnaces and Steel Mills	7.79	10.20	13.99	1.18	1.65	2.42	2.03	2.76	6.18
2869 Industrial Organic Chemicals, N.E.C.	6.21	6.76	11.74	0.69	0.93	1.91	–	D	3.86
2621 Papermills, Except Building, Paper	7.23	7.96	12.32	1.04	1.23	2.28	–	–	–
2631 Paperboard Mills	7.35	8.46	12.19	0.92	1.18	2.12	–	–	–
3241 Cement, Hydraulic	8.79	9.33	13.85	0.92	1.10	2.02	–	S	D
3334 Primary Aluminum	3.42	4.26	5.59	0.67	0.74	D	–	–	D
2812 Alkalies and Chlorine	5.46	5.92	10.08	0.89	0.90	1.80	–	4.18	–
2824 Synthetic Organic Fibers, Except Cellulosic	6.38	7.83	12.35	1.07	1.25	2.65	–	–	–
2865 Cyclic Intermediates and Crudes	N/A	9.27	11.88	N/A	1.19	2.40	N/A	–	–
3221 Glass Containers	8.50	9.33	14.99	1.38	1.64	2.58	–	–	–
3714 Motor Vehicle Parts and Accessories	10.28	11.65	17.27	1.86	1.96	3.02	4.80	D	11.31
3711 Motor Vehicles and Passenger Car Bodies	9.80	11.40	18.44	1.68	1.96	2.90	–	–	10.94

Source: Authors' estimates based on U.S. Deaprtment of Commerce, Bureau of the Census, *Annual Survey of Manufacturers 1974: Fuels and Electric Energy Consumed* (Washington, D.C.: U.S. Government Printing Office, 1976). U.S. Department of Commerce, Bureau of the Census, *1972 Census of Manufacturers: Fuels and Electric Energy Consumed* (Washington, D.C.: U.S. Department of Commerce, Bureau of the Census, 1973). U.S. Department of Commerce, Bureau of the Census, *1967 Census of Manufacturers: Fuels and Electric Energy Consumed* (Washington, D.C.: U.S. Government Printing Office, 1971).

Notes: Average dollar costs does not reflect other fuels and fuels not specified by kind (NSK). N/A = not available; D = data withheld to avoid identification of individual firms; S = data withheld, because estimates do not meet Bureau of Census standards for publication; – = zero.

Table 3-3
Energy Efficiency in 1967, 1971, and 1974

Industry	Consumption/Output			Percent Change		Compound Annual Rate of Change	
	1967	1971	1974	1967-1971	1971-1974	1967-1971	1971-1974
All Manufacturers	34.614	36.569	31.574	5.65	-13.66	1.38	-4.78
2911 Petroleum Refining	3.865	3.885	3.583	0.52	- 7.77	0.13	-2.65
3312 Blast Furnaces and Steel Mills	4.156	4.257	3.839	2.43	- 9.82	0.60	-3.39
2869 Industrial Organic Chemicals, N.E.C.	2.325	2.108	1.910	- 9.32	- 9.39	-2.43	-3.22
2621 Papermills, Except Building, Paper	1.487	1.497	1.287	0.70	-14.03	0.16	-4.91
2631 Paperboard Mills	1.259	1.082	1.086	-14.06	0.37	-3.72	0.12
3241 Cement, Hydraulic	1.366	1.204	1.246	-11.84	3.49	-3.11	1.15
3334 Primary Aluminum	0.863	0.704	0.737	-18.38	4.68	-4.97	1.54
2812 Alkalies and Chlorine	0.544	0.446	0.433	-17.94	- 2.92	-4.84	-0.98
2824 Synthetic Organic Fibers, Except Cellulosic	0.257	0.261	0.194	1.56	-25.67	0.39	-9.42
2865 Cyclic Intermediates and Crudes	N/A	0.321	0.246	N/A	-23.36	N/A	-8.49
3221 Glass Containers	0.346	0.359	0.325	3.76	- 9.22	0.93	-3.26
3714 Motor Vehicle Parts and Accessories	0.310	0.317	0.315	2.26	- 0.63	0.55	-0.21
3711 Motor Vehicles	0.347	0.292	0.287	-15.85	- 1.71	-4.22	-0.57

Source: Authors' estimates based on Federal Reserve Systems, Board of Governors, *Industrial Production Indexes*, various issues; *Annual Survey of Manufacturers 1974; 1972 Census of Manufacturers; 1967 Census of Manufacturers*. U.S. Department of Commerce, Bureau of Census, *Annual Survey of Manufacturers 1974: Fuels and Electric Energy Consumed* (Washington, D.C.: U.S. Government Printing Office, 1976). U.S. Department of Commerce, Bureau of the Census, *1972 Census of Manufacturers: Fuels and Electric Energy Consumed* (Washington, D.C.: U.S. Government Printing Office, 1973). U.S. Department of Commerce, Bureau of the Census, *1967 Census of Manufacturers: Fuels and Electric Energy Consumed* (Washington, D.C.: U.S. Government Printing Office, 1971).

Notes: Energy efficiency is calculated by dividing KHEs of total purchased energy consumption by the appropriate FRB Index. N/A = not available.

in 1971 and then by another 40 percent to $13.80 per 1000 KHEs in 1974. The higher prices resulted both from a heavier reliance on fuel oil relative to other fuels in generating electricity and from the rise in fuel oil prices already discussed.

Coal usage declined from 17 percent of total purchased energy consumption in 1967 to 12 percent in 1971 and 9 percent in 1974. Much of this decline can be attributed to the increased costs of extracting, transporting, handling, and burning coal that resulted from environmental and pollution controls. As Table 3-2 shows, the average dollar cost of coal in manufacturing as a whole rose by 46 percent from $0.96 per 1000 KHEs in 1967 to $1.40 per 1000 KHEs in 1971 and then by another 107 percent to $2.95 per 1000 KHEs in 1974. The true cost of burning coal rose much more than these figures indicate, of course, because of the extensive capital investments in scrubbers and other pollution control equipment required to burn coal.[f]

Natural gas usage increased from 47 percent of total purchased energy consumption in 1967 to 51 percent in 1971, but then decreased to 49 percent in 1974. This peaking reflects peak load curtailments during winter heating seasons and the difficulty of obtaining new hook-ups more than it does the effect of higher natural gas prices. Although the average dollar cost of natural gas rose by 20 percent from $1.09 per 1000 KHEs in 1967 to $1.31 per 1000 KHEs in 1971 and then by another 72 percent to $2.25 per 1000 KHEs in 1974, natural gas remained considerably cheaper than other fuels.

The Thirteen Individual Industries

Although the patterns of energy consumption in the thirteen largest energy-consuming industries varied widely, the changes in these patterns during the 1967-1974 period were broadly consistent with those already described for manufacturing as a whole. Such consistency is hardly surprising, of course, inasmuch as the thirteen industries accounted for about half of total purchased energy consumption in manufacturing as a whole throughout the 1967-1974 period.[g]

As Table 3-1 shows, total purchased energy consumption increased in nine of twelve industries from 1967 to 1974. Those industries experiencing the largest relative rises in total purchased energy consumption between 1967 and 1974 were: synthetic organic fibers, SIC industry 2824; industrial organic chemicals, SIC industry 2869; primary aluminum, SIC industry 3334; and glass containers,

---

[f]Government mandated efforts to substitute coal for oil as a boiler fuel are likely to increase coal usage in the future, although the extent of the increase cannot be determined yet.

[g]The three largest energy consuming industries—blast furnaces, SIC industry 3312; petroleum refining, SIC industry 2911; and industrial organic chemicals, SIC industry 2869— accounted for approximately 30 percent of total purchased energy consumed in manufacturing as a whole in 1974.

SIC industry 3221. Total purchased energy consumption increased in six of twelve industries from 1967 to 1971 and in eight of thirteen industries from 1971 to 1974. Total purchased energy consumption rose more or declined less from 1967 to 1971 than from 1971 to 1974 in six industries; the opposite occurred in six industries.

Distillate and residual oil usage rose as a percent of total purchased energy consumption in ten of twelve industries and eight of ten industries, respectively, from 1967 to 1974. The share of distillate oil usage rose in more industries from 1967 to 1971 than from 1971 to 1974, while the share of residual oil usage rose in slightly fewer industries from 1967 to 1971 than from 1971 to 1974.

Electricity usage rose as a percent of total purchased energy consumption in all thirteen industries from 1967 to 1974. In only two industries did it fail to increase steadily both from 1967 to 1971 and from 1971 to 1974. In many industries the rise in reliance on electricity was dramatic, possibly reflecting a relative decline in coal usage from 1967 to 1974 and a relative decline in natural gas usage from 1971 to 1974.

Coal usage declined steadily as a percent of total purchased energy from 1967 to 1971 and from 1971 to 1974 in all industries for which data are available. Physical consumption of coal also declined steadily in all but four industries throughout the 1967–1974 period. Natural gas usage rose as a percent of total purchased energy consumption in nine of twelve industries from 1967 to 1971, but then fell in eight of twelve industries from 1971 to 1974.

As Table 3-2 shows, average dollar cost per 1000 KHEs of total purchased energy consumption rose faster in all industries from 1971 to 1974 than from 1967 to 1971. Most industries appear to have reacted to this accelerated inflation in energy prices by using energy more efficiently. As Table 3-3 indicates, only six of twelve industries improved their energy efficiency ratios from 1967 to 1971, while ten of thirteen industries did so from 1971 to 1974.

Explaining the Pattern Changes

Production theory posits a positive relationship between changes in factor inputs and changes in output, while demand theory posits an inverse relationship between the price and quantity demanded of a good. Operation of these two theories appears to have played a fundamental role in determining purchased energy consumption patterns in the manufacturing sector during the 1967–1974 period. Total purchased energy consumption grew proportionately with output from 1967 to 1971 when energy prices were relatively stable, but grew much more slowly than output from 1971 to 1974 when energy prices rose rapidly. Similarly, the fuel mix of total purchased energy consumption changed as the prices of specific fuels changed relative to one another.

It is beyond the scope of this chapter to try to explain fully the changes in purchased energy consumption patterns that occurred in the manufacturing sector from 1967 to 1974. However, the information in Tables 3-1 through 3-3 does permit a preliminary examination of the changes in total purchased energy consumption that occurred in the thirteen largest energy-consuming industries using the reduced form equation

$$\%\Delta E = a + b\,\%\Delta Q - c\,\%\Delta P \qquad (3.1)$$

where $\%\Delta E$ is the percent change in total purchased energy consumption in each industry, $\%\Delta Q$ is the percent change in the FRB index for each industry, and $\%\Delta P$ is the percent change in average dollar cost per 1000 KHEs of total purchased energy consumption in each industry.[h]

Using ordinary least squares (OLS) to estimate Equation (3.1) with pooled data for both 1967–1971 changes and 1971–1974 changes yields the regression

$$\%\Delta E = \begin{array}{ccc} .010 & + \ .790\,\%\Delta Q - & .087\,\%\Delta P, \\ (.19) & (5.07) & (-1.50) \end{array}$$

$$R^2 = .52; \text{No. of obs.} = 24 \qquad (3.2)$$

with t-statistics reported in parentheses below the coefficients. The coefficient on $\%\Delta Q$ is significantly different from zero at the .005 confidence level and not significantly different from one. Thus, this coefficient cannot be said to demonstrate that total purchased energy rose less rapidly than output between 1967 and 1974 even though it has a value of less than one. The coefficient on $\%\Delta P$ has the appropriate negative sign, but is not significant. This coefficient could reflect a lagged response to prices that does not show up in Equation (3.2), because the major price rises between 1967 and 1974 occurred late in the period.

Using OLS to estimate Equation (3.1) with data for 1967–1971 changes gives the regression

$$\%\Delta E = \begin{array}{ccc} .029 & + \ 1.129\,\%\Delta Q - & .420\,\%\Delta P, \\ (.16) & (4.89) & (-.64) \end{array}$$

$$R^2 = .70; \text{No. of obs.} = 11 \qquad (3.3)$$

Once again the coefficient on $\%\Delta Q$ is significant at the .005 confidence level,

---

[h]Equation (3.1) is estimated as a cross-section using the thirteen individual industries as the observations. Equation (3.1) should not be interpreted as a demand equation, because it ignores the identification problem that arises from the simultaneous determination of demand and supply.

but is now slightly greater than one. The negative coefficient on $\%\Delta P$ is now smaller in absolute value than before, which probably reflects the stability of energy prices during the 1967-1971 period. Equation (3.3) shows clearly that changes in output exerted the dominant influence on total purchased energy consumption between 1967 and 1971, a period characterized by relatively stable energy prices.

Using OLS to estimate Equation (3.1) with data for 1971-1974 changes results in the regression

$$\%\Delta E = .144 + .428 \,\%\Delta Q - .156 \,\%\Delta P$$
$$ (1.52) \quad (2.04) \qquad (-1.50) \tag{3.4}$$

$$R^2 = .18; \text{No. of obs.} = 13$$

Here the coefficient on $\%\Delta Q$ is significantly different from both zero and one at the .05 confidence level. The negative coefficient on $\%\Delta P$ is still insignificant but does have a larger t-statistic than before. Together, these coefficients indicate that rapidly rising energy prices may have discouraged total purchased energy consumption between 1971 and 1974, with the price increases occurring too late in the period to play a statistically significant role in Equation (3.4).

The fact that Equation (3.4) has much less explanatory power than Equations (3.2) and (3.3) and the fact that Equation (3.4) has the only coefficient on $\%\Delta Q$ significantly less than one suggest that different forces may have determined total purchased energy consumption between 1967 and 1971 than between 1971 and 1974. Comparing Equations (3.3) and (3.4) with a Chow test fails to corroborate this hypothesis, however. It gives an F-statistic of 2.37 (3, 18), which is insignificant at the .10 confidence level. Total purchased energy consumption appears to have changed proportionally to output in the 1967-1971 period and less than proportionally to output in the 1971-1974 period, because energy prices were stable during the first period and rising rapidly during the second one.

References

1. The Conference Board. *Energy Consumption in Manufacturing* (Cambridge: Ballinger Publishing Co., 1974).

2. U.S. Department of Commerce, Bureau of the Census. *Annual Survey of Manufacturers 1974: Fuels and Electric Energy Consumed* (Washington, D.C.: U.S. Government Printing Office, 1976).

3. U.S. Department of Commerce, Bureau of the Census. *1972 Census of Manufacturers: Fuels and Electric Energy Consumed* (Washington, D.C.: U.S. Government Printing Office, 1973).

4. U.S. Department of Commerce, Bureau of the Census. *1967 Census of Manufacturers: Fuels and Electric Energy Consumed* (Washington, D.C.: U.S. Government Printing Office, 1971).

4 The Impact of Higher Oil Prices on Economic Growth in the Industrial Economies
Peter Morici, Jr.

Introduction

Following the outbreak of the October 1973 Middle East War, OPEC implemented an unanticipated threefold increase in the real price of crude oil. This increase had significant impacts on the levels of economic activity in the oil importing industrial economies. It changed the structures of relative prices, induced structural changes in production and consumption, and altered paths of economic growth. This chapter surveys the impacts of higher oil prices on the paths of economic growth in the Western industrial economies.

The chapter is divided into three main sections. The first section discusses on a theoretical level the impacts of higher oil prices on economic growth in the industrial economies. The second section describes the economic climate just prior to the Middle East war, summarizes the policy responses of the major industrial countries to supply curtailments and higher oil prices, and surveys several empirical studies which consider the short-run impacts of higher oil prices. The third section reports the results of studies which analyze the long-run impacts of higher oil prices on the industrial countries.

Theoretical Analysis[a]

The real crude oil price increases imposed by the OPEC cartel had impacts similar to an excise tax imposed on crude oil in the typical oil importing economy. In this case the tax was imposed by an external authority, OPEC, that did not inject the tax revenues back into the economy through transfers or additional expenditures. As a result, real income and wealth were transferred from the oil importing country to OPEC. In addition, the higher price of imported oil caused increases in the prices of domestic energy sources in the typical oil importing country, transferring real wealth and income within the country from users to owners of energy resources.[b]

The author wishes to thank Arthur J. Malloy, E. Stanley Paul, and the editor for their helpful comments and encouragement. The responsibility for errors remains the author's.

[a]Basevi; Fried and Schultze; Gunning, Osterrieth, and Waelbroeck; and Mussa have included theoretical discussions of this problem in [1], [3], [4], and [7].

[b]These transfers of wealth and income were limited to the extent that domestic price controls limited price increases. It is assumed that prices were allowed to rise to eliminate shortages in the analysis below. Energy prices did rise significantly when OPEC increased its prices, minimizing shortages in the industrial countries.

35

The Short Run

In the short run, the increases in the price of imported oil and the cost of domestic energy sources caused an increase in the absolute price level. This decreased real disposable income and the real value of consumer wealth, thereby depressing consumption expenditures and aggregate demand. Also, the increase in the cost of energy caused a shift in purchases of consumer durables away from those intense in the use of energy, such as automobiles.[c]

The increased prices of domestic energy sources created expanded investment opportunities and the profits needed to finance such investment. However, to the extent that the additional profits realized by the domestic energy sector were not distributed as additional dividends or spent on additional investment activity, they contributed to the reduction in aggregate demand. Most domestic energy firms found it difficult to undertake additional investment in the short run.[d]

The higher price of imported oil had serious impacts on the foreign sector of the typical oil importing country. It increased the cost of oil imports and reduced exports to other oil importing countries as they experienced the depressing effects of the higher price of imported oil. These developments reduced the nominal value of the net trade balance, which in turn had multiplier effects on aggregate demand. To the extent that OPEC translated the increased revenues it received from oil, into additional imports, such effects on the nominal value of the net trade balance were tempered. However, the surpluses that OPEC accumulated in its current accounts indicate that it did not increase imports as much as oil revenues would have allowed.

The Long Run

Higher oil prices have already induced increases in the relative prices of all domestic energy forms, causing changes in production and consumption patterns, as households and firms seek energy substitutes. These adjustments will tend to make real GNP lower than it otherwise would have been in terms of the price structure which prevailed before the real price of imported oil tripled. The real GNP loss imposed by these changes in relative prices will be smaller than the net welfare loss imposed on the economy.

The net welfare loss and the real GNP reduction caused by higher energy prices, assuming full employment and external equilibrium, may be examined

---

[c]See [13, pp. 91–92].

[d]Perry found changes in investment owing to higher oil prices minimal for the United States in the short run; see [13, pp. 92–93].

with the aid of the standard supply and demand framework used to evaluate the impact of a tariff.[e] Figure 4-1 shows the domestic supply and demand for energy in a typical oil importing economy. The economy is assumed to face a fixed import price expressed in terms of other goods. At the precartel world energy price, P_0, the economy produces Q_0 energy and imports Q_0Q_1 energy. At the cartel energy price, P_1, the economy expands production to Q_2 and reduces imports to Q_2Q_3. Consumers surplus decreases by $A + B + C + D + E$

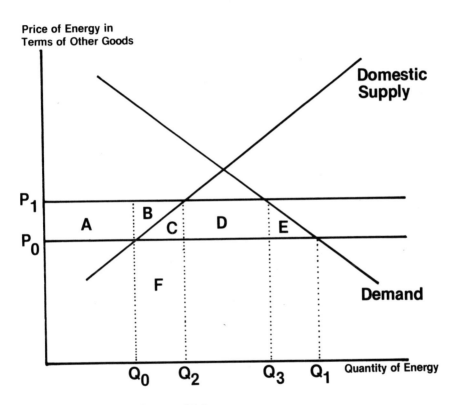

Figure 4-1. Impacts of a Cartel Price

---

[e]The comparative static analysis employed here is an interpretation of the long-run analysis of Fried and Schultze in [3, pp. 43–56]. They did not employ the supply and demand apparatus in their analysis. The analysis is presented here for generalized primary energy rather than for oil as in the Fried and Schultze discussion. The analysis applies when relative prices have been changed by a tariff, subsidy, quota, or equivalent action, but not when relative prices have been altered by a change in the resource base or technical change. For a similar analysis, see [1, pp. 134–36].

because of the increase in the world energy price. $C + D + E$ is the net welfare loss to society, because $A + B$ is a transfer from energy consumers to domestic energy producers. C is the resource cost of producing $Q_0 Q_2$ energy instead of importing it at precartel prices, that is, the efficiency loss associated with producing more domestic energy. D is the additional cost of importing $Q_2 Q_3$ energy because of the higher cartel price. E represents the consumption cost of conserving energy. Shared by firms that use energy as an intermediate input and by households that purchase energy for final consumption, E reflects the costs incurred by firms that substitute other inputs for energy in production processes and the utility losses experienced by households that reduce energy consumption.[f]

Fried and Schultze contend that part of the net welfare loss constitutes a real GNP loss.[g] C, the efficiency loss in the production of additional energy, is the increased resource cost of extracting energy from a fixed supply of land. Diverting these resources from the production of other goods lowers real GNP.[h] D, the additional payment for importing $Q_2 Q_3$ energy, is necessitated by the change in the terms of trade and does not reduce the production of final goods and services. Therefore, D does not represent a reduction in real GNP. That part of E corresponding to the efficiency costs incurred by firms that switch to less energy-intense modes of production lowers productivity and real GNP, *ceterus paribus*. However, that part of E representing the utility losses experienced by households that reduce energy consumption does not show up in real GNP and cannot lower it.

The real GNP losses associated with the production of additional energy and the substitution of energy used as an input in production processes arise only at precartel relative prices. Consider first the real GNP loss associated with C. At precartel prices, $C + F$ resources are required to produce $Q_0 Q_2$ energy, whereas F resources are required to produce the other goods necessary to trade for the same amount of energy. Real GNP is reduced by the difference, C, when domestic energy is substituted for imported energy. At cartel prices $C + F$ resources are required to produce $Q_0 Q_2$ energy domestically, while $B + C + F$ resources are required to produce the other goods necessary to trade for the same amount of energy. Here producing $Q_0 Q_2$ energy domestically instead of

---

[f]If the good in question were used only as an intermediate product, then E would only represent the efficiency loss borne by the producers of other goods. If the imported good in question were used only as a final consumption good, then E would only represent the utility lost by households from a reduction in final energy consumption.

[g]See [3, pp. 53–54].

[h]This assertion is based on the assumption that full employment is maintained. To produce larger amounts of domestic energy, resources must be diverted from the production of other goods. To say that real GNP is reduced requires a comparison of the other goods forgone with the newly produced energy. A vector of relative prices is necessary for such a comparison. At precartel prices the energy obtained by expanding production ($Q_0 Q_2$) is valued less than the other goods sacrificed to obtain the additional energy. This is explored further below.

trading for it results in a real GNP gain. Now consider that part of E which represents the efficiency loss incurred by firms because of the substitution of other inputs for energy in production processes. Assume firms select the minimum cost combinations of labor, capital, energy, and other material inputs to produce other goods at the precartel price of energy. Creation of the cartel alters this relative price structure, causing firms to substitute for energy with other inputs. Although the new combination of inputs is more costly and less efficient at precartel relative prices, it minimizes costs and is efficient at cartel relative prices.

In addition to the impacts of higher energy prices on real GNP just discussed, higher energy prices may have an impact on real GNP in the long run by affecting the size of the capital stock. Economic activity and investment are initially reduced by higher energy prices. The size of the capital stock and the levels of real GNP will be reduced in the future if the lost investment expenditures are not made up at a later date. Some sectors of the economy will contract, while others will expand, as relative prices change, discouraging investment in the contracting sectors and encouraging it in the expanding ones. OPEC investments of its current account surpluses in the industrial countries will increase capital accumulation to some extent, offsetting some of the initial decline, but these investments are likely to be channeled to those industrial countries that offer the most promising investment opportunities and are least in need of the external funds.

Short-term Impacts

The Economic Climate Prior to the Middle-East War

In October 1973 the major industrial economies were experiencing above-average growth. The average growth rates in 1972 and 1973 for Canada, the United States, Japan, France, West Germany, Italy, and the United Kingdom were 5.8 percent and 6.5 percent, respectively, compared to 5.3 percent during the previous twelve years. The aggregate industrial production index for members of the Organization for Economic Cooperation and Development (OECD) rose 19 percent on a seasonally adjusted basis from 1971:1 to 1973:3[i]

Despite this rapid growth, unemployment continued to be a serious problem in 1972 and 1973. In Canada, West Germany, France, and the United Kingdom the civilian unemployment rate in the first three quarters of 1973 was above the average for the previous ten years. In the United States it bottomed

---

[i]The growth rates are averages of percent changes in real GNP and real GDP for the countries mentioned; see Table 1 in [8, p.9]. Values for the industrial production index were taken from an OECD computer tape.

out in the second half of 1973 at 4.7 percent, the 1962–1972 average and a dis-appointing level for the peak of a cycle. In Italy the civilian unemployment rate for the second half of 1973 averaged 3.1 percent which was below the 1962–1972 average of 3.4 percent.[j]

Inflation in the industrial countries accelerated during the two years pre-ceding the embargo. A fundamental factor in that acceleration was the rapid increase in the world prices of oil, minerals, and agricultural products.[k] Con-tributing to the increases in the prices of primary commodities were the strong demand conditions created by the synchronization of economic activity in the industrial economies, the crop failures of 1972, and the bargaining power OPEC was gaining in its dealings with the international oil companies. Between early 1970 and June 1, 1973, the f.o.b. price of Saudi Arabia marker crude oil at Ras Tanura increased by about 80 percent in real terms to $2.70 per barrel.[l]

Policy Responses to Supply Curtailments and Higher Oil Prices

On October 6, 1973, war broke out in the Middle East. Ten days later the Persian Gulf nations announced posted price increases which raised the f.o.b. price of Saudi Arabian marker crude oil to $3.65 per barrel. On October 21, the Arab oil producers embargoed the United States and the Netherlands and announced 5 percent to 10 percent curtailments in crude oil production. On November 4, these curtailments were increased to 25 percent. The Arab nations expressed their intention that friendly nations receive normal supplies of oil, with other nonembargoed nations sharing the balance of the shortfall not borne by the United States and the Netherlands. However, the international oil com-panies reallocated their non-Arab supplies to spread the shortage more evenly. In late December the production curtailments were reduced to 15 percent. During the period between October 16, 1973, and January 1, 1974, the f.o.b. price of Saudi Arabian marker crude oil increased to $9.66 per barrel.[m]

Western Europe. Although the announcement of production cutbacks by Arab oil exporters in 1973 created a great deal of concern in Western Europe about shortages, the shortages did not turn out to be as severe as expected. Several non-Arab nations increased exports; price increases led to consumption reductions;

---

[j]See Table 6 in [9, p. 28].

[k]For a complete analysis of the impact of higher commodity prices on world inflation and an account of the commodity price boom of 1973–1974, see [8, pp. 25–37].

[l]See [20, p. 229].

[m]See [20, pp. 229–32, 234].

and conservation measures had some effect. Conservation measures included bans on Sunday driving, speed limit reductions, and gasoline rationing, with emphasis placed on keeping industrial needs supplied to maintain employment. The conservation measures did not do nearly as much as did increases in petroleum prices to reduce consumption.

The Western European governments were unable to agree on a program to allocate crude oil among the various countries. Instead, the major oil companies controlling the majority of crude oil entering Europe allocated oil in response to market forces. Belgium, the Netherlands, Italy, Spain, and the United Kingdom imposed controls on exports of refined petroleum products. However, the oil companies were able to route oil through refineries in other countries as needed. Countries allowing price increases received oil, while those restraining prices suffered more. The West German government received authority from parliament in November 1974 to regulate prices, but relied on "jawboning" to keep petroleum product price increases from becoming excessive. This approach allowed imports to the extent the West German people were willing to pay higher prices. In contrast, France regulated prices, thereby discouraging heating oil imports from the Netherlands.[n]

Petroleum product shortages did not significantly reduce the level of economic activity, because higher oil prices—and to a lesser extent conservation measures—kept serious shortages from materializing. The OPEC production curtailments affected economic activity mainly through the impacts that higher oil prices had on aggregate demand.

Japan. Japan depends on imports for most of its raw materials. Consequently, it is especially vulnerable to disruptions and wide price swings in world raw materials markets. Imported oil accounts for over 70 percent of its primary energy requirements. Despite considerable Japanese pessimism about the availability of oil early in the embargo, the Arab production curtailments had their primary impacts on aggregate demand through higher oil prices and the uncertainty the production curtailments created.

Soon after the Arab oil embargo began, concern arose about devaluation of the yen, balance of payment difficulties, a continuation of doubt digit inflation, and reduced industrial production. Legislation imposing direct controls on major commodity prices and the consumption of oil and electric power was adopted. In early 1974 the government began to allow relative price changes reflecting the higher oil prices. At the end of March a phasing out of controls was begun by allowing petroleum product prices to rise an average of 62 percent.[o]

---

[n]Discussions of the events outlined in the preceding two paragraphs may be found in [1, pp. 125–28], [6, pp. 78–83], and [16, pp. 100–1].

[o]See [19, pp. 145–49].

United States. The situation in the United States differed from that in most oil importing countries, because the United States is a significant producer as well as importer of oil. Therefore, it had greater price control options than did other importing nations when faced with the embargo and price increases. The United States chose a middle course between regulating crude oil prices and allowing them to reach a level determined by market forces. A two-tier pricing system defined in terms of 1972 production levels was adopted for domestic oil in September 1973.[p] The price of "old" oil was set at $5.03 per barrel in December of that year, while the price of "new" oil was allowed to find its own level. The two-tier pricing policy had a significant impact on refinery acquisition costs: the average refiner acquisition cost of crude oil increased significantly during the embargo period, but not by nearly as much as the increase in the cost of imported oil.

Allocation and conservation programs were implemented to deal with shortages created by the embargo. The basic thrust of the allocation program was to supply industry and commerce, keep homes heated, and have the motoring public bear the principal burden of petroleum product shortages. This policy was successful in preventing industrial shutdowns due to fuel shortages.[q] Industries dependent on private motorists for their business—such as automobile repair shops and resorts—were affected by shortages of gasoline, however, and some industries were depressed by uncertainty concerning the future of energy supplies. The primary impact of the embargo on the U.S. economy came from the impact of higher energy prices on aggregate demand.[r]

Macroeconometric Studies

Economic growth slowed and inflation accelerated in the oil importing countries after the onset of the Middle East war. The average rate of economic growth in the OECD countries fell from 5.4 percent over the 1960–1972 period and 6.3 percent in 1973 to 0.3 percent in 1974. The average rate of increase in consumer prices rose from 4.7 percent in 1972 and 7.7 percent in 1973 to 14.1 percent for the twelve-month period beginning in October 1973.[s] Several studies have used macroeconometric models to determine how much of these changes were the result of the 1973–1974 oil crisis.

---

[p]See [13, p. 77–81].

[q]See [13, p. 83].

[r]See [13, p. 88].

[s]The economic growth rates are averages of both real GNP and real GDP changes. The 1960–72 average and 1973 data are from Table 1 in [10, p. 13]; the 1974 value is from Table 1 in [11, p. 11]. The price data are from Table 14 in [9, p. 42].

OECD. To measure the relative impacts of higher oil prices on the OECD countries, Schwartz employed a regional system of identically structured models for the United States, Canada, Japan, West Germany, France, Italy, Belgium-Luxembourg, the Netherlands, the United Kingdom, the rest of OECD, and a simpler model for the rest of the nonsocialist world.[t] Keynesian in structure, the models have equations for consumption, investment, exports, and imports, but do not include a monetary sector. The system links the individual models through trade flows; without product disaggregation and with exchange rates assumed constant. All equations are specified in percent change terms and have parameters that are elasticities, permitting Schwartz to evaluate the impacts of an exogenous shock specified in percent change terms with a single simulation. Schwartz simulated his regional system to estimate the impacts of a 233 percent increase in the price of oil exported by non-OECD nations. The average GDP change in OECD after four years was 3.5 percent, equivalent to a 0.9 percentage point reduction in growth rates. The greatest and smallest decreases in GDP were 8 percent in Italy and 0.4 percent in the United States.[u]

Western Europe. Basevi performed two sets of calculations with impact multipliers that Hickman developed from the Project LINK system of macroeconometric models to estimate the impacts of higher oil prices on Western Europe.[v] Each set of calculations was performed in four stages. First, Basevi estimated the increase in oil import costs, the increase in exports to OPEC, and the decrease in exports to the non-oil exporting developing countries that the increases in the price of OPEC oil gave rise to. Second, he calculated the impacts of these changes on real GNP in the United States, Japan, and Western Europe with impact multipliers which do not consider foreign trade feedback effects. Third, he calculated the feedback effects that reduced economic activity in the United States and Japan had on Western European exports and real GNP. Fourth, he added the real GNP impacts obtained in the third step to the real GNP impacts obtained in the second step to calculate the total impacts of higher oil prices to real GNP Western Europe. In his first set of calculations Basevi found real GNP losses of 2.66 percent, 2.89 percent, 2.82 percent, and 1.91 percent in 1974, 1975, 1976, and 1977, respectively. In a second set of

---

[t]See [17].

[u]The other countries experienced the following GDP losses: Canada 4.0 percent, Japan 5.2 percent, Belgium-Luxembourg 7.8 percent, France 7.2 percent, West Germany 7.1 percent, Netherlands 4.3 percent, United Kingdom 6.0 percent, and the rest of OECD 7.3 percent; see [17, pp. 10-1].

[v]Western Europe is defined here as the European members of the OECD: Austria, Belgium, Denmark, Finland, France, West Germany, Greece, Iceland, Ireland, Italy, Luxembourg, the Netherlands, Norway, Portugal, Spain, Sweden, Switzerland, Turkey, and the United Kingdom. See[1].

calculations, where he incorporated World Bank estimates of the increases in investment expected in the United States, Japan, and Western Europe as a result of higher oil prices into the first stage calculation described above, Basevi found real GNP losses of 2.38 percent, 2.14 percent, and 1.30 percent in 1974, 1975, and 1976, respectively, and a real GNP gain of 0.03 percent in 1977.[w]

Japan. Watanabe performed three simulations with an econometric model of Japan to measure the impacts of the oil crisis on that country.[x] The first simulation assumed no oil crisis and demand management policies less restrictive than those actually in force after October 1973. The second simulation assumed no oil crisis and the restrictive monetary and fiscal policies actually in force after October 1973. The third simulation assumed the oil prices and demand management actually in force after October 1973. Comparing the second and third simulations shows the impacts of higher oil prices net of any demand management changes. The annual rate of real GNP change between fiscal years 1972 and 1974 was 5.5 percent in the second simulation and 3.0 percent in the third simulation. The annual rate of consumer price change was 10.4 percent in the second simulation and 19.3 percent in the third simulation. Comparing the first and third simulations shows the impacts of higher oil prices if the restrictive demand management policies put in force after the onset of the oil crisis are viewed as a result of higher oil prices.[y] The annual rates of real GNP and consumer price change were 7.4 percent and 10.6 percent, respectively, in the first simulation. Both comparisons indicate that higher oil prices were a contributing factor, but not the sole cause of slower growth and more rapid inflation in Japan during the embargo and postembargo period.

As a separate exercise, Watanabe compared simulation based on a real crude oil price in 1974 dollars of $10 per barrel through 1977 with a simulation based on a real crude oil price in 1974 dollars gradually declining from $10 per barrel in 1974 to $6 per barrel in 1977. With the first of these two simulations the annual rates of change in real GNP were 2.1 percent, 4.2 percent and 7.9 percent in 1975, 1976, and 1977, respectively. With the second of these two simulations, the comparable rates were 3.4 percent, 4.7, percent and 8.7 percent. These results support the argument that higher oil prices reduced economic growth in Japan.

United States. Several studies have been undertaken to measure the short-term impacts of higher oil prices on the U.S. economy.[z] An FEA study based on the

---

[w]As Basevi noted, neither set of calculations included the depressing effects that increases in the price of coal had on aggregate demand in Europe. See [1, pp. 106–16].

[x]See [19].

[y]Monetary and fiscal policy might well have been less restrictive toward the end of 1973 and during 1974 in the absence of the oil crisis, because the House of Counselors was scheduled for election in July 1974. See [19, pp. 149–50].

[z]Several such studies are reviewed by David Serot in Chapter 2 of this volume. Also see [14].

Data Resources, Inc. (DRI) model compared a high oil price simulation designed to track the energy crisis with a counterfactual low oil price simulation eliminating its effects.[aa] Several adjustments were made to the exogenous inputs of the high oil price simulation to generate the low price simulation: eliminating dummy variables associated with the embargo; assuming that unit value indexes for crude oil and petroleum products imports and the wholesale price index for fuels and related products and power grow at their preembargo rates; removing the postembargo supplemental import fees; adjusting the constant dollar value of imported petroleum products downward. The constant dollar value of federal government expenditures and monetary policy were assumed to be unaffected by higher oil prices. In another study, Perry compared similar high oil price and low oil price simulations performed with the Federal Reserve Board (FRB) and University of Michigan models.[bb]

Table 4-1 summarizes the results of the FEA and Perry studies for 1975:4, two years after the embargo. Real GNP was lower in the high oil price simulations than in the low oil price simulations with both studies, indicating losses ranging from 3.1 percent to 8.2 percent because of the energy crisis.[cc] By 1975:4 the losses in 1958 dollars were $66.9 billion, $24.9 billion, and $37.5 billion with the DRI, FRB, and University of Michigan models, respectively. In the FEA study, real GNP declined during 1974 in both the high oil price and low oil price simulations. It declined from $830.4 billion in 1974:1 to $777.2 billion in 1975:1 with the high oil price simulation, and from $838.1 billion in 1974:3 to $817.7 billion in 1975:1 with the low oil price simulation. This result suggests that higher oil prices increased the depth of the 1974–1975 recession, but were not its sole cause. The real GNP implicit price deflator was also higher in the high oil price simulations than in the low oil price simulations with both studies, indicating that the energy crisis also accelerated inflation.

Long-term Impacts

Few empirical studies examining the long-term impacts of higher oil prices have been produced to date. The shortage of studies reflects both the difficulties involved in constructing and specifying new models to evaluate the long-term impacts and the relatively short time that has elapsed since the onset of the energy crisis. Forecasting the principal long-term impacts of higher oil prices

---

[aa]See [12].

[bb]See [13].

[cc]The losses are calculated relative to a real GNP level of $815.5 billion in 1958 dollars, the 1975:4 level in the FEA high oil price simulation. Perry did not report real GNP levels. In part, Perry's simulations indicated smaller impacts than the FEA simulations, because he did not consider the depressing effects of higher oil prices on other countries. He estimated that this difficulty may have reduced his impact estimates by as much as 20 percent. See [13, pp. 102–3].

Table 4–1

1975:4 Real GNP, Prices, and Unemployment in the FEA and Perry Studies

	FEA		Perry
	(DRI)	(FRB)	(University of Michigan)
Real GNP			
Differences between high oil price and low oil price simulations in billions of 1958 dollars	−66.9	−24.9	−37.5
GNP Implicit Price Deflator			
Percent differences between high oil price and low oil price simulations	6.74	2.4	4.8
Unemployment Rate			
Differences between high oil price and low oil price simulations	2.5	1.6	1.7

Sources: Office of Energy Information and Analysis, Federal Energy Administration, *Report to Congress on the Economic Impact of Energy Actions*, NTIS PB-256-684 (Springfield, Va.: National Technical Information Center, 1976), Table 1, p. 8; George L. Perry, "The United States," in Fried and Schultz, eds., *Higher Oil Prices and the World Economy*, pp. 96–97. Perry's results are available through 1977:4.

Note: The original Perry study stated real GNP changes in 1973 dollars.

requires forecasting the effects that changes in relative prices have on the quantities of various goods produced, the use of energy in production processes, and the long-run capital stock. OPEC investments in the industrial countries and short-run reductions in aggregate demand and investment caused by higher oil prices are also important to the extent that they affect the capital stock. At least two studies have used models with some of these desirable capabilities to examine the long-term impacts of higher oil prices in industrial countries.[dd]

The U.S. delegation to the Conference on International Economic Cooperation, held in April 1976, presented a paper containing estimates of the impacts of higher oil prices on the U.S. economy.[ee] These estimates were generated with the Wharton Long-term Annual and Industry Forecasting Model, a large-scale macroeconometric model containing an imbedded input-output matrix with price sensitive input substitution coefficients.[ff] The study concluded that real

---

[dd]In addition, two other studies have examined the impacts of new energy technologies and alternative government policies on economic growth in the U.S. See [2] and [5].

[ee]See [18].

[ff]The price sensitive input substitution coefficients enable the model to capture many of the long-run effects discussed above. Their validity is restricted by the assumption that the elasticity of substitution is identical between all pairs of material inputs. However, this assumption does not generally hold for energy versus nonenergy inputs. For a description of the model, see [15].

GNP in 1974 dollars would be reduced between $79 billion and $118 billion in 1980 by higher oil prices. This impact represents a 1980 real GNP reduction between 5.2 percent and 7.8 percent and a 1974-1980 growth rate reduction between 0.7 and 1.1 percentage points.

Gunning, Osterrieth, and Waelbroeck formulated a supply-oriented growth model of the OECD emphasizing the energy sector.[gg] Using the assumption that labor is fully employed, the model was specifically designed to capture the effects of higher oil prices on the amount of energy produced within the OECD, the amount of energy used in production processes, the level of investment, and the recycling of OPEC current account surpluses into the OECD. Gunning, Osterrieth, and Waelbroeck performed a simulation assuming the price of imported oil to be $3.21 in 1973 dollars and another simulation assuming it to be $8.19 in 1973 dollars. The rate of growth in OECD real national income for the 1973-1980 period was 4.37 percent with the former simulation and 4.21 percent with the latter simulation, a difference of 0.16 percentage points. The rate of growth in OECD real national income for the 1980-1985 period was 4.43 percent with the former simulation and 4.37 percent with the latter simulation, a difference of 0.06 percentage points. These differences may understate the actual impacts of higher oil prices on economic growth, because the model does not capture the depressing effects that higher oil prices have on aggregate demand and investment in the short run.

Conclusions

The threefold increase in the world price of crude oil which followed the outbreak of the 1973 Middle East War has significantly affected price levels and economic activity in the industrial countries. In the short run, higher energy prices acted much like an excise tax, raising the general price level and depressing aggregate demand in the typical industrial country. These developments lengthened and deepened postembargo recessions in most countries.

In the long run higher oil prices will also have impacts on the level and composition of real GNP in the typical industrial country by changing the structure of relative prices and affecting the capital stock. Changes in relative prices will induce changes in the relative importance of various sectors, encourage energy conservation, and spur the development of additional domestic energy resources. Investment will rise in some sectors and fall in others. The short-term depressing effects of higher oil prices on aggregate demand and investment will reduce the capital stock and real GNP in the long run if the investment expenditures lost in the short run are not made up. Finally, the recycling of OPEC current account surpluses may have a positive impact on investment in some sectors, offsetting some of the negative effects of higher imported oil prices.

[gg]See [4].

The evidence presented in the previous section indicates that the combined effects of these factors on the level of economic activity is likely to be negative through 1985.

References

1. Basevi, Giorgio. "Western Europe." In Fried and Schultze, eds., *Higher Oil Prices and the World Economy: The Adjustment Problem* (Washington, D.C.: The Brookings Institution, 1975), pp. 105-42.

2. Carter, Anne P. "Energy, Environment, and Economic Growth." *Bell Journal of Economics and Management Science* 5, no. 2 (Autumn 1974), pp. 578-92.

3. Fried, Edward R. and Charles L. Schultze. "Overview." In Fried and Schultze, eds., *Higher Oil Prices and the World Economy: The Adjustment Problem* (Washington, D.C.: The Brookings Institution, 1975), pp. 1-69.

4. Gunning, J.W., M. Osterrieth, and J. Waelbroeck. "The Price of Energy and the Potential Growth of Developed Countries." *European Economic Review*, no. 7 (1976), pp. 35-62.

5. Hudson, Edward A. and Dale E. Jorgenson. "U.S. Energy Prices and Economic Growth, 1975-2000." *Bell Journal of Economics and Management Science* 5, no. 2 (Autumn 1974), pp. 461-514.

6. Menderhausen, Horst. *Coping with the Oil Crisis* (Baltimore, Md.: Johns Hopkins University Press, 1974).

7. Mussa, Michael. "Oil, Relative Prices, and Macroeconomic Policy in an Open Economy." Mimeographed, Unviersity of Rochester, November 1974.

8. OECD. *Economic Outlook*, no. 15 (July 1974).

9. OECD. *Economic Outlook*, no. 16 (December 1974).

10. OECD. *Economic Outlook*, no. 17 (July 1975).

11. OECD. *Economic Outlook*, no. 19 (July 1976).

12. Office of Energy Information and Analysis, Federal Energy Administration. *Report to Congress on the Economic Impact of Energy Actions.* NTIS PB-256-684 (Springfield, Va.: National Technical Information Center, 1976).

13. Perry, George L. "The United States." in Fried and Schultze, eds., *Higher Oil Prices and the World Economy: The Adjustment Problem* (Washington, D.C.: The Brookings Institution, 1975), pp. 71-104.

14. Pierce, John, and Jared Enzler. "The Effects of External Inflationary Shocks." *Brookings Papers of Economic Activity*, no. 1 (1974), pp. 13-54.

15. Preston, Ross S. *The Wharton Annual and Industry Forecasting Model* (Philadelphia, Pa: Economic Research Unit, University of Pennsylvania, 1972).

16. Prodi, Romano, and Alberto Clô. "Europe." in Vernon, ed., *The Oil Crisis* (New York: W.W. Norton, 1976), pp. 91–112.

17. Schwartz, A. N. R. *The Effects of the Rise in Oil Prices on the Economy of the Industrialized Countries.* Monograph no. 17, The Netherlands Central Planning Bureau, 1974.

18. "Impact of the 1973/1974 Oil Price Increase on the United States Economy to 1980." Paper presented by the United States in the Energy Commission at the Conference on International Economic Cooperation, April 21, 1976, Paris.

19. Watanabe, Tsunehiko. "Japan." In Fried and Schultze, eds., *Higher Oil Prices and the World Economy: The Adjustment Problem* (Washington, D.C.: The Brookings Institution, 1975), pp. 143–67.

20. Yeager, Joseph A., and Eleanor B. Steinberg. "Trends in the International Oil Market." In Fried and Schultze, eds., *Higher Oil Prices and the World Economy: The Adjustment Problem* (Washington, D.C.: The Brookings Institution, 1975), pp. 227–75.

5

Effects of the Energy Policy and Conservation Act on Energy Independence and the National Economy
A. Bradley Askin and Richard L. Farman

Introduction

In his January 1975 State of the Union message to Congress, President Ford out-lined an energy program which would "begin to restore our country's surplus capacity in total energy."[a] As part of this program Mr. Ford asked that within ninety days Congress decontrol the price of domestic crude oil, enact a windfall profits tax on oil producers, deregulate natural gas, and establish excise taxes and fees of $2 per barrel on all imports of crude oil and refined petroleum products.

A week after his State of the Union address, Mr. Ford imposed supple-mentary oil import fees on imports of crude oil and refined petroleum products as the first step in implementing his program. These fees were to become effec-tive in three stages: $1 per barrel starting on February 1, $2 per barrel starting on March 1, and $3 per barrel starting on April 1. In late February, Congress passed a bill to suspend for ninety days the president's authority to impose oil import fees. Mr. Ford vetoed this legislation, but postponed the supplementary fees scheduled to go into effect on March 1 and April 1 until May 1 and June 1, respectively, to allow Congress sixty days for deliberation as it had requested. On June 1 Mr. Ford put the $2 supplementary fees into effect, but never insti-tuted the $3 fees.

Although he had initially proposed immediate decontrol of domestic crude oil prices, President Ford amended this stance three times during the spring and summer. In April he suggested that decontrol be phased in over a two-year period; in mid-July he stretched the decontrol period to thirty months; finally, at the end of July he lengthened the decontrol period to thirty-nine months. Congress rejected each of these modified decontrol proposals on the grounds that they would raise energy prices too rapidly, thereby accelerating inflation and exacerbating unemployment. The Democratic majority in Congress called for a five-year period of phased decontrol combined with mandatory conserva-tion measures and other regulations to minimize the impacts of higher energy prices on consumers. Mr. Ford rejected this approach.

A previous version of this paper was presented under another title at the Third Annual University of Missouri, Rolla-Missouri Energy Council Conference on Energy held in Rolla, Missouri, October 12–14, 1976.

[a]See [5, p. 48].

Existing price controls on domestic crude oil temporarily lapsed at the end of August when the Emergency Petroleum Allocation Act (EPAA) expired. Congress passed an extension of the EPAA, but the president vetoed it to keep Congress under pressure to act on decontrol. In early September, after the Senate failed in an attempt to override the EPAA veto, the president and Congress agreed to work toward a decontrol compromise, and the EPAA was extended for sixty days.

During September and October, members of the Ford administration met with members of Congress on a variety of House-Senate conference bills after the two houses of Congress passed separate legislation. In November, after the EPAA had again been temporarily extended, members of the administration and the House-Senate conferees reached agreement on a forty-month phased decontrol package. This compromise plan was sent to Mr. Ford on December 18 and signed into law by him as the Energy Policy and Conservation Act (EPCA) on December 22.

The energy program imbedded in the EPCA departed significantly from that originally proposed by the president nearly a year earlier. Decontrol of domestic crude oil prices was to occur gradually, following the establishment of an initial average price of $7.66 per barrel.[b] Neither a windfall profits tax nor natural gas deregulation was enacted. The EPCA contained no provision for excise taxes and fees on imports of crude oil and refined petroleum products; in fact, as part of the compromise with Congress, Mr. Ford removed the $2 per barrel supplementary fees imposed in June 1975.

In this chapter we examine the economic consequences of the EPCA. Our purpose is to assess both the extent to which the EPCA could be expected to meet the stated objective of restoring energy self-sufficiency and the impacts it could be expected to have on the national economy as of late 1975 and early 1976. The next section summarizes the main provisions of the EPCA. The following sections describe the methodology we have used to analyze the EPCA and report the results of our analysis. The final section presents our conclusions.

Provisions of the EPCA

The EPCA, signed into law by President Ford on December 22, 1975, provides for phased decontrol of domestic crude oil over a forty-month period beginning February 1, 1976. It consists of five major sections dealing with a variety of matters in addition to decontrol. Portions of the EPCA are superseded by the Energy Conservation and Production Act (ECPA), signed into law in August 1976.

---

[b]The members of the Ford administration and the House-Senate conferees who worked out the EPCA compromise package thought the average price of domestic crude oil then in effect net of taxes and fees was $7.66 a barrel. In fact, it was higher than that.

Title I of the EPCA addresses the availability and development of domestic energy supplies. It grants the administrator of the FEA authority to guarantee loans for the development of new underground coal mines subject to a stringent set of eligibility requirements. It also directs the administrator to establish and maintain a strategic petroleum reserve designed to lessen the impacts of severe energy supply interruptions. Other provisions prohibit joint bidding by major oil companies for the rights to develop offshore oil fields and establish allocation and export restrictions on equipment and materials used in developing and producing domestic crude oil and natural gas.

Title II of the EPCA gives the president specific standby authorities that can be implemented in the event of a severe energy supply interruption or to comply with obligations under international energy agreements. Authority is granted to impose rationing and implement one or more contingency plans that would restrict energy consumption. Such contingency plans are required to have the prior approval of Congress.

Title III of the EPCA sets forth energy efficiency standards. It establishes fuel economy standards for certain classes of motor vehicles and provides heavy penalties for noncompliance with these standards. Title III also mandates targets for improving the energy efficiency of major appliances and certain other consumer products.

Title IV of the EPCA establishes a domestic crude oil pricing policy to be implemented in three stages. First stage implementation establishes a maximum weighted average first sale price of $7.66 per barrel on domestic crude oil effective February 1, 1976. This initial ceiling price is approximately $0.87 per barrel lower than the average price of domestic crude oil which prevailed in January 1976. Second stage implementation gives the president authority to raise the ceiling price in subsequent months to offset the effects of inflation and provide an incentive for enhancing domestic crude oil production. Adjustment as a production incentive is limited to a 3 percent annual rate; adjustment to offset inflation and as a production incentive is limited to a 10 percent annual rate. Third stage implementation allows the president to submit to Congress amendments that would relax the limits on the rate at which the ceiling price may be raised. The need for the proposed amendments to provide an adequate incentive for sustaining or improving domestic crude oil production must be documented in any such submission.

Title V of the EPCA grants broad authorities to federal agencies to verify information reported by the energy industry. These authorities include the power to subpoena and examine books, records, and documents kept by companies engaged in the production, transportation, processing, or distribution of energy resources. The Securities and Exchange Commission is directed to prescribe accounting procedures to be used by companies producing crude oil or natural gas so as to facilitate the compilation of a reliable energy data base.

The ECPA, also known as the FEA Extension Act, amends the EPCA in a variety of ways, most of which need not be considered here. With respect to pricing, it changes the EPCA Title IV policy by partially decontrolling stripper and tertiary crude oil prices. The ECPA allows stripper and incremental tertiary crude oil to sell at the world price of crude oil rather than at the price of "new" domestic crude oil, with stripper crude oil treated as if it sells at the price of "new" domestic crude oil when computing the EPCA Title IV ceiling price of domestic crude oil.

Methodology

In cooperation with others at the FEA, we performed four separate analyses during late 1975 and 1976 to determine the economic effects of the EPCA.[c] The first analysis, initiated prior to passage of the EPCA, examined the economic implications of the proposed EPCA pricing provisions relative to a continuation of the status quo. The second and third analyses, undertaken after the adoption of the EPCA, analyzed the economic impacts of the EPCA provisions at various stages of implementation. The final analysis, undertaken prior to passage of the ECPA, analyzed the effects of the ECPA amendments to the EPCA Title IV pricing policy.

Each of the four analyses relied upon a common methodology using two separate models to measure the impacts of alternative energy scenarios. Energy sector impacts were estimated with the Short-Term Petroleum Forecasting System (STPFS) developed at the FEA. Outputs from the STPFS were then used as inputs for simulations with the 1975 version of the DRI macroeconomic model to determine the corresponding impacts on the national economy.

The STPFS operated in a stepwise manner. First, forecasts for domestic production of crude oil and natural gas liquids were generated. Then, price estimates were derived for various refined petroleum products based on these production estimates and assumptions concerning the world price of crude oil, import duties, and domestic price regulations. Next, the price estimates were used in an econometric demand model with forecasted macroeconomic data to determine the domestic demand for eight different refined petroleum products. Finally, imports of crude oil and refined petroleum products were estimated as the residuals in identities involving domestic demands, domestic production, and changes in domestic stocks.[d]

The values of four variables in a standard DRI model simulation were modified on the basis of STPFS simulation results to create a macroeconomic

---

[c]Three of these analyses are reported on in [4], [6], and [7]. The ECPA analysis is available only in the form of internal FEA memoranda.

[d]For a complete description of the STPFS and the solution procedure for it, see [1].

simulation for each alternative energy scenario: the wholesale price index for fuels and related products and power, the 1967 constant dollar values of imported crude oil and refined petroleum products, and the average unit value index for imported crude oil. Only the wholesale price index for fuels and related products and power was directly estimated by the STPFS. New values for the 1967 constant dollar values of imported crude oil and refined petroleum products were obtained by multiplying the STPFS estimated volumes of imported crude oil and refined petroleum products times their respective 1967 customs average unit value prices. The average unit value index of imported crude oil was obtained by dividing the STPFS estimated price of imported crude oil, net of import fees, by its 1967 customs average unit value price. Since fees on imported crude oil were incorporated into the standard DRI simulation used, indirect business taxes were reduced to reflect the elimination of such fees when appropriate.[e]

Empirical Results

Table 5-1 summarizes the major assumptions underlying six scenarios that can be used to assess the consequences of the EPCA for energy sector demand and supply conditions and for the national economy. The scenarios "Pre-EPCA I"

Table 5-1
Major Assumptions for EPCA Scenarios

Scenario	Constraints on Domestic Crude Oil Prices	Supplementary Fees on Imports of Crude Oil and Refined Petroleum Products	World Price of Crude Oil
Pre-EPCA I	"Old" oil controlled at $5.25/bbl	$2.00/barrel	Constant in real terms
	"New" oil uncontrolled; remains constant in real terms		
Pre-EPCA II	Same as above	None	Same as above
EPCA Stage I	Average price controlled at $7.66/bbl	None	Same as above
EPCA Stage II	Average price set at $7.66/bbl February 1, 1976, then increases 10 percent annually	None	Same as above
EPCA Stage III	Average price set at $7.66/bbl February 1, 1976, then increases 14 percent annually	None	Same as above
S&T Decontrol	Average price set at $7.66/bbl February 1, 1976, then increases 10 percent annually; stripper and tertiary oil partially decontrolled	None	Same as above

[e]More detailed descriptions of the DRI model and our energy scenario simulation procedure are available in [2], [3], and Chapter 7 of this volume.

and "Pre-EPCA II" reflect the state of the world before the EPCA became effective. The $2 per barrel supplementary fees imposed by President Ford on imports of crude oil and refined petroleum products are assumed to continue indefinitely in the former scenario and be eliminated January 1, 1976, in the latter scenario. The scenarios "EPCA Stage I," "EPCA Stage II," and "EPCA Stage III" reflect the states of the world after successive stages of implementation of the EPCA Title IV pricing policy. The scenario "S&T Decontrol" corresponds to the state of the world implied by partial decontrol of stripper and incremental tertiary crude oil under the ECPA.

The six scenarios in Table 5-1 were assembled from the four separate studies referred to in the previous section and analyzed with the methodology described in that section. Inasmuch as modifications were made in the STPFS between the times that the four separate studies were conducted, some of the results presented in them are not directly comparable. Fortunately, the "EPCA Stage II" scenario was considered in all four studies and serves as a common reference point among them. Thus, the comparability problem can be minimized by using the "EPCA Stage II" scenario as a base case and analyzing all other scenarios relative to it.

Table 5-2 reports the estimated energy sector impacts on domestic crude oil prices and imports of crude oil and refined petroleum products through 1978 for all other scenarios relative to the "EPCA Stage II" scenario. Similarly, Table 5-3 reports the estimated macroeconomic impacts on the Consumer Price Index (CPI), real GNP, and the unemployment rate through 1978 for all other scenarios relative to the "EPCA Stage II" scenario.[f]

Table 5-2 shows that domestic crude oil prices are lower after first stage EPCA implementation than without the EPCA. As can be seen from the "Pre-EPCA II" scenario, however, eliminating the supplementary import fees actually accounts for about one-half of the impact that the initial rollback of domestic crude oil prices appears to have in the "Pre-EPCA I" scenario. Subsequent stages of EPCA implementation then gradually offset the effects of the initial rollback on domestic crude oil prices and leave them at levels comparable to those of the pre-EPCA situation with supplementary fees.

There are only small differences in imports of crude oil and refined petroleum products among scenarios.[g] The maximum variation between any two scenarios in the share of domestic consumption of refined petroleum products

---

[f]The forty-month EPCA decontrol program extends into 1979, but forecast horizon limitations of the STPFS did not allow us to extend simulations past 1977 in some cases and 1978 in others. In addition to minimizing the comparability problem, reporting differences among scenarios rather than levels has the advantage of de-emphasizing the particular assumptions for exogenous variables underlying the standard DRI simulation used.

[g]Domestic crude oil production was assumed to be the same in the "EPCA Stage I" and "EPCA Stage III" scenarios as in the "EPCA Stage II" scenario. Thus, differences between imports of crude oil and refined petroleum products in these scenarios only reflect changes in domestic energy demand. Domestic crude oil production does vary in other scenarios relative to the "EPCA Stage II" scenario.

Table 5-2
Energy Sector Impacts Relative to the "EPCA Stage II" Scenario

a. Differences in the Average Price of Domestic Crude Oil ($/bbl)

	1976	1977	1978
Pre-EPCA I (Fees)	1.54	1.62	NA
Pre-EPCA II (No Fees)	0.79	0.68	NA
EPCA Stage I	−0.29	−1.09	−1.56
EPCA Stage III	0.11	0.45	1.08
S&T Decontrol	0.22	0.92	0.83

b. Differences in Imports of Crude Oil and Refined Petroleum Products (MMB/day)

	1976	1977	1978
Pre-EPCA I (Fees)	−0.32	−0.43	NA
Pre-EPCA II (No Fees)	−0.23	−0.31	NA
EPCA Stage I	0.01	0.07	0.13
EPCA Stage III	−0.01	−0.02	−0.07
S&T Decontrol	−0.01	−0.12	−0.28

c. Percentage Point Differences in Imports of Crude Oil and Refined Petroleum Products as a Percent of Domestic Consumption of Refined Petroleum Products

	1976	1977	1978
Pre-EPCA I (Fees)	−1.0	−2.0	NA
Pre-EPCA II (No Fees)	−1.0	−2.0	NA
EPCA Stage I	0.0	1.0	0.0
EPCA Stage III	0.0	0.0	−1.0
S&T Decontrol	0.0	−1.0	−2.0

Source: Authors' estimates, based on Richard L. Farman, "Economic Effects of Relaxing the EPCA Ceiling Price Adjustment Limits on Domestic Crude Oil," Working Paper 76-WPA-36, National Impact Division, Office of Macroeconomic Impact Analysis, Federal Energy Administration, (June 1976): National Impact Division, "Analysis of the Effects of Adjusting the $7.66 Per Barrel Ceiling Price of Domestic Crude Petroleum at a 10 Percent Compounded Annual Rate," Working Paper 76-WPA-10, Office of Macroeconomic Impact Analysis, Federal Energy Administration, (February 1976): Office of Macroeconomic Impact Analysis and Office of Oil and Gas, "Analysis of the Effects of the Energy Policy and Conservation Act," Working Paper 76-WPA-25, Federal Energy Administration, (February 1976); and internal FEA memoranda.

met by imports of crude oil and refined petroleum products is only 3 percentage points. This lack of response in imports to changes in energy policy and domestic crude oil prices can be attributed to the price inelasticity of energy demand in the short run and the long lead times required to significantly increase domestic energy supply.

The macroeconomic impacts of the EPCA reflect primarily the effects that changes in domestic energy prices have on the aggregate price level. The reduction in domestic energy prices after first stage EPCA implementation relative to the pre-EPCA scenarios leads to a reduction in consumer prices as measured by the CPI. In turn, the lower consumer prices stimulate aggregate demand, as measured by real GNP, and reduce the unemployment rate relative to the pre-EPCA scenarios. Subsequent stages of EPCA implementation cause

Table 5-3

Macroeconomic Impacts Relative to the "EPCA Stage II" Scenario

a. Percent Differences in the Consumer Price Index

	76:1	76:2	76:3	76:4	77:1	77:2	77:3	77:4	78:1	78:2	78:3	78:4
Pre-EPCA I (Fees)	0.3	0.4	0.5	0.7	0.9	1.0	1.1	1.1	NA	NA	NA	NA
Pre-EPCA II (No Fees)	0.2	0.2	0.2	0.3	0.4	0.4	0.4	0.4	NA	NA	NA	NA
EPCA Stage I	0.0	0.0	-0.1	-0.1	-0.1	-0.2	-0.3	-0.3	-0.4	-0.5	-0.6	-0.7
EPCA Stage III	0.0	0.0	0.0	0.0	0.1	0.1	0.1	0.1	0.2	0.2	0.2	0.2
S&T Decontrol	0.0	0.0	0.0	0.1	0.1	0.2	0.2	0.3	0.3	0.3	0.3	0.3

b. Differences in Real GNP in Billions of 1958 Dollars (Percent Differences in Parentheses)

	76:1	76:2	76:3	76:4	77:1	77:2	77:3	77:4	78:1	78:2	78:3	78:4
Pre-EPCA I (Fees)	-1.6 (-0.20)	-2.5 (-0.30)	-3.8 (-0.45)	-5.7 (-0.66)	-8.1 (-0.92)	-10.2 (-1.16)	-12.5 (-1.40)	-14.4 (-1.60)	NA	NA	NA	NA
Pre-EPCA II (No Fees)	0.6 (0.07)	-0.3 (-0.04)	-0.6 (-0.07)	-1.3 (-0.15)	-2.1 (-0.24)	-2.9 (-0.33)	-3.7 (-0.41)	-4.3 (-0.47)	NA	NA	NA	NA
EPCA Stage I	0.0 (0.00)	0.1 (0.01)	0.2 (0.03)	0.5 (0.06)	0.9 (0.11)	1.5 (0.17)	2.3 (0.25)	3.4 (0.38)	4.6 (0.50)	6.1 (0.66)	7.5 (0.82)	8.9 (0.96)
EPCA Stage III	0.0 (0.00)	0.0 (0.00)	-0.1 (-0.01)	-0.2 (-0.02)	-0.4 (-0.04)	-0.6 (-0.07)	-0.9 (-0.10)	-1.4 (-0.15)	-1.8 (-0.20)	-2.3 (-0.26)	-2.8 (-0.31)	-3.2 (-0.35)
S&T Decontrol	0.0 (0.00)	0.0 (0.00)	0.0 (0.00)	-0.1 (-0.01)	-0.1 (-0.01)	-0.4 (-0.05)	-1.2 (-0.13)	-2.2 (-0.25)	-2.5 (-0.28)	-3.2 (-0.35)	-3.1 (-0.34)	-2.8 (-0.31)

c. Percentage Point Differences in the Unemployment Rate

	76:1	76:2	76:3	76:4	77:1	77:2	77:3	77:4	78:1	78:2	78:3	78:4
Pre-EPCA I (Fees)	0.0	0.1	0.1	0.2	0.2	0.3	0.4	0.5	NA	NA	NA	NA
Pre-EPCA II (No Fees)	0.0	0.0	0.0	0.0	0.1	0.1	0.1	0.1	NA	NA	NA	NA
EPCA Stage I	0.0	0.0	0.0	0.0	0.0	0.0	-0.1	-0.1	-0.1	-0.2	-0.2	-0.3
EPCA Stage III	0.0	0.0	0.0	0.0	0.0	0.0	0.0	0.0	0.1	0.1	0.1	0.1
S&T Decontrol	0.0	0.0	0.0	0.0	0.0	0.0	0.0	0.0	0.1	0.1	0.1	0.1

Source: Authors' estimates, based on Richard L. Farman, "Economic Effects of Relaxing the EPCA Ceiling Price Adjustment Limits on Domestic Crude Oil," Working Paper 76-WPA-36, National Impact Division, Office of Macroeconomic Impact Analysis, Federal Energy Administration, (June 1976); National Impact Division, "Analysis of the Effects of Adjusting the $7.66 Per Barrel Ceiling Price of Domestic Crude Petroleum at a 10 Percent Compounded Annual Rate," Working Paper 76-WPA-10, Office of Macroeconomic Impact Analysis, Federal Energy Administration, (February 1976); Office of Macroeconomic Impact Analysis and Office of Oil and Gas, "Analysis of the Effects of the Energy Policy and Conservation Act," Working Paper 76-WPA-25, Federal Energy Administration, (February 1967); and internal FEA memoranda.

consumer prices to rise over time as phased decontrol occurs, gradually off-setting most of the impacts that first stage implementation has on real GNP and unemployment relative to the pre-EPCA situation.[h]

Conclusions

The analysis presented here indicates that the forty-month phased decontrol program set forth in Title IV of the EPCA and modified by the EPCA could be expected as of late 1975 and early 1976 to have little impact on either U.S. energy independence or the general economy through 1978. On the one hand, these results are disappointing, because they provide no basis for crediting the forty-month decontrol program with alleviating U.S. dependence on foreign energy sources. Dependence on foreign oil is just as high under all four decontrol scenarios examined as under either of the pre-EPCA scenarios considered. On the other hand, the results are reassuring, since they imply that gradual decontrol of domestic crude oil prices has little impact on either consumer prices and the rate of inflation or real output and the rate of unemployment.

The most striking aspect of the results is the role played by the removal of the $2 supplementary fees on imports of crude oil and refined petroleum products as part of the EPCA compromise. For the short-run period considered, eliminating these fees has negligible adverse effects on energy autarky, while having favorable impacts on the national economy that are larger in magnitude than the impacts found for any other scenario.

Although the decontrol of domestic crude oil prices attracted most of the attention during the year-long debate between the Ford administration and Congress that preceded enactment of the EPCA, our analysis of the Title IV pricing provisions suggests that they will not significantly alter the status quo with respect to U.S. dependence on OPEC and other foreign sources of petroleum. The legacy of the EPCA appears more likely to spring from other, less publicized portions of the act than from Title IV.

References

1. Alt, Christopher B. *National Petroleum Product Supply and Demand, 1976-1978*, NTIS-PB-254-969 (Springfield, Va.: National Technical Information Service, 1976).

---

[h]The major role played by domestic energy prices in determining the macroeconomic impacts reflects two important aspects of the analysis. First, domestic energy supply and demand remain virtually constant over the short time horizon considered, as mentioned above. Consequently, the effects of policy changes on domestic energy prices are not muted by changes in the quantities of energy demanded and supplied. Second, the DRI model relies heavily upon energy prices to capture the effects that perturbations in the energy sector have on the national economy.

2. Askin, A. Bradley. "The Macroeconometric Implications of Alternative Energy Scenarios." In Askin and Kraft, eds., *Econometric Dimensions of Energy Demand and Supply* (Lexington, Mass.: D.C. Heath and Co., 1976), pp. 91–109.

3. Data Resources, Inc. "The Data Resources Quarterly Model" (May 1975).

4. Farman, Richard L. "Economic Effects of Relaxing the EPCA Ceiling Price Adjustment Limits on Domestic Crude Oil." Working Paper 76-WPA-36, National Impact Division, Office of Macroeconomic Impact Analysis, Federal Energy Administration (June 1976).

5. Ford, Gerald R. "The State of the Union." In *The Weekly Compilation of Presidential Documents*, 2, no. 3 (Washington, D.C.: Office of the Federal Register, National Archives and Records Service, General Services Administration, January 20, 1975).

6. National Impact Division. "Analysis of the Effects of Adjusting the $7.66 Per Barrel Ceiling Price of Domestic Crude Petroleum at a 10 Percent Compounded Annual Rate." Working Paper 76-WPA-10, Office of Macroeconomic Impact Analysis, Federal Energy Administration (February 1976).

7. Office of Macroeconomic Impact Analysis and Office of Oil and Gas. "Analysis of the Effects of the Energy Policy and Conservation Act." Working Paper 76-WPA-25, Federal Energy Administration (February 1976).

6

Simulating Alternative Energy Scenarios with the Wharton Long-term Model of the U.S. Economy
Arthur J. Malloy

Introduction

The Arab oil embargo of 1973-1974 and the quadrupling of foreign crude oil prices between 1973 and 1974 were significant factors contributing to recent U.S. economic difficulties. These events have served to underscore the importance of the energy sector in shaping general economic conditions. Accordingly, quantitative studies of the macroeconomic impacts of potential energy developments are essential for formulating sound energy policies.

The Federal Energy Administration (FEA) has developed and used a system of energy models known as the Project Independence Evaluation System (PIES) to simulate the energy sector implications of alternative energy scenarios.[a] PIES has been used to examine a wide range of assumptions concerning the configuration of domestic energy supply and demand, domestic energy policies, and the price of foreign crude oil. Among other variables, PIES projects the levels of domestic production, consumption, imports, and prices of all major energy forms.

By incorporating PIES energy sector forecasts into a large macroeconomic model, it is possible to simulate the macroeconomic impacts of a broad spectrum of energy scenarios.[b] Previous FEA macroeconometric simulations have used the Data Resources, Inc. (DRI) and Chase Econometric Associates, Inc. (Chase) model of the U.S. economy. Energy prices and imports have provided the major inputs from PIES in these simulations. Since both the DRI and Chase models are demand oriented and structured around the final demand categories of the National Income Accounts, these studies have largely ignored PIES forecasts

The author is grateful to William Rice for his contributions to all phases of this study. Richard Farman made several useful comments on an earlier version, and A. Bradley Askin provided some valuable methodological insights. Last, but not least, staff members of Wharton Econometric Forecasting Associates and Boeing Computer Services provided data assistance and the margin of victory in some minor skirmishes of the war between man and machine.

[a]Results of PIES simulations of several energy scenarios and descriptions of PIES are contained in [5] and [6].

[b]See [2] for a general discussion of other macroeconomic simulations of PIES energy scenarios.

of domestic energy production and consumption.[c] As a result, price changes induced by supply shifts have not been distinguished from those induced by demand shifts.[d]

In contrast to the DRI and Chase models, both output and price variables for substantially disaggregated industries are integral parts of the Wharton Annual and Industry Model. Because the model contains separate functions explaining investment in twenty-nine producing sectors, it also captures changes in energy and nonenergy investment associated with changes in energy prices and production.

This chapter uses the Wharton model to estimate the macroeconomic effects of fourteen PIES scenarios in order to take advantage of these features.[e] The first section of the chapter describes the methodology used to simulate the PIES scenarios with the Wharton model. Discussions of the macroeconomic simulation results and the conclusions of the study follow in the next two sections.

Methodology

General Procedures

The Wharton Annual and Industry Model was used to simulate the macroeconomic implications of fourteen energy scenarios based on the Wharton control solution of December 18, 1975. Prior to each simulation, this control solution was modified using PIES forecast data for the relevant scenario. Comparisons of the simulation results provided estimates of the macroeconomic impacts of the different scenarios.

Two major problems arose in connection with the incorporation of PIES information into the Wharton model. First, since no PIES variables appear explicitly in the model, PIES data could not be directly substituted into the model.[f] It was necessary to use variables in the Wharton model which were related to one or more PIES variables as entry points for the PIES data. This required the formulation of linkages to determine the value of each entry point

---

[c]Some studies have incorporated PIES projections of gasoline consumption through adjustments of real personal consumption expenditures for gasoline and oil. However, these expenditures account for an insignificant portion of final demand and play a minor role in the simulations.

[d]See [2, pp. 96-97]. In Chapter 7 of this volume, Farman and Lagace point out that this is not a serious problem in the DRI model when the relevant energy form is imported and its price is not regulated.

[e]The Wharton Annual and Industry Model is described in [7] and [15].

[f]The term "PIES data" as used here includes arithmetic transformations of PIES variables.

variable from the values of the related PIES variables. These linkages are discussed in detail below.

Second, PIES generally provided forecasts for 1985 only, while the Wharton model had to be solved annually over the entire simulation period, starting in 1974.[g] Values of the entry point variables for each year from 1975 to 1985 were generated on the assumption that the PIES variables grow at a constant compound annual rate from 1974 to 1985.[h]

For each scenario, the values of thirteen variables in the Wharton control solution were modified to reflect PIES data. These included the values of four domestic output variables, two domestic price variables, one domestic consumption variable, three import quantity variables, and three import price variables. To ensure maximum consistency with PIES, endogenous variables generally were exogenized at levels determined by the PIES linkages. However, since the output variables in the Wharton model could not be exogenized, adjustments to the constant terms in the equations explaining these variables were used to modify their Wharton control solution values. The constant terms were adjusted by the differences between the values of the output variables as determined with the PIES linkages and their values in the Wharton control solution.

Specific Procedures

Output. The Wharton model divides the supply side of the economy into sixty-three producing sectors. Each sector includes one or more two-digit Standard Industrial Classification (SIC) industry groups. Output in each sector is measured by the total of the 1958 dollar values of the gross products originating in the industry groups included.

Of the sixty-three producing sectors in the Wharton model, energy accounts for a significant share of output in Coal Mining; Oil and Gas Extraction; Petroleum Refining and Related Industries; and Electric, Gas, and Sanitary Services. The Wharton variables representing the total real gross products originating in these four sectors—XMG11+12, XMG13, XMFN29, and XRGU49, respectively—were linked to PIES projections of energy production in physical units.[i]

---

[g]The simulations were run in May 1976 and used the version of the model and the control solution that were then current. Owing to delays in the benchmark revisions of the National Income Accounts (NIA), the 1974 values of some of the NIA variables in the model were not available when the control solution was prepared. Consequently, 1974 was part of the "forecast" period in the control solution. As will be seen below, the simulations used the 1974 control solution values of all macroeconomic variables.

[h]Unless otherwise noted, 1974 and other historical values of all energy variables were obtained from [4].

[i]The numerical suffix appended to each variable contains the two-digit SIC codes of the industry groups it includes. See [3] for a detailed description of the industry groups.

Since XMG11+12 includes only one PIES energy form, and does not include any other goods or services, linking this variable to the 1985 PIES forecast of coal production was straightforward. Using 1974 historical data and the 1985 PIES forecast of coal production, the average annual rate of growth in coal production was calculated for each scenario. This growth rate then was applied to the 1974 Wharton control solution value of XMG11+12 to obtain values of this variable from 1975 to 1985.

XMG13, XMFN29, and XRGU49 all include other goods and services in addition to PIES energy forms. Each of these variables was treated as a sum of real gross products originating from the production of individual PIES energy forms and other goods and services.

A three-step procedure was used to convert PIES physical production data into real gross products originating from the production of individual PIES energy forms within SIC groups 13, 29, and 49. First, the 1974 Wharton control solution value of each of the three output variables—XMG13, XMFN29, and XRGU49—was allocated to individual PIES energy forms on the basis of the historical importance of each energy form in the value of the output of the relevant producing sector.[j] This allocation provided estimates of the real gross products originating from the production of individual PIES energy forms in 1974. Second, the average annual rate of growth in the production of each energy form between 1974 and 1985 was calculated using 1974 historical data and 1985 PIES data. Third, these growth rates were applied to the corresponding 1974 estimates to generate real gross products originating from the production of individual PIES energy forms from 1975 through 1985.

Given the 1974 estimates of the real gross products originating from the production of PIES energy forms in SIC groups 13, 29, and 49, the remainders of the 1974 control solution values of XMG13, XMFN29, and XRGU49, respectively, were assigned to the production of other goods and services. Depending on the types of other goods and services included in a particular output variable, one of two procedures was used to generate real gross product originating from the production of other goods and services from 1975 through 1985. Because the other goods and services included in XMG13—natural gas liquids and gas and oil field services—are closely related to crude petroleum and natural gas, the remainder of XMG13 was adjusted to grow at the same rate as the combined real gross product originating from the production of crude petroleum and natural gas. In contrast, the other goods and services included in XMFN29 and

---

[j]The 1972 share of each PIES energy form in the value of shipments of SIC group 13 was used to allocate the 1974 control solution value of XMG13. For each of the other two groups, the 1972 share of each PIES energy form in total value added was used. Data on SIC group 13 were obtained from [9, p. 3], [10, p.5], and [11, p. 4]. Data on SIC group 29 were obtained from [12, pp. 6-7]. Unpublished estimates of the 1972 shares of PIES energy forms in total value added in SIC group 49 were obtained from the Bureau of Economic Analysis, U.S. Department of Commerce.

XRGU49 are not closely related to PIES energy forms. Accordingly, the remainder of each of these variables was adjusted to grow at the same compound annual rate as the control solution value of the variable itself.

Domestic Prices. PIES provides forecasts of the domestic prices of all major energy forms in 1985. The variables in the Wharton model which are closest conceptually to product prices are implicit deflators for the gross products originating in twenty-nine producing sectors. Because the model disaggregates output into sixty-three producing sectors, there is not a one-to-one correspondence between price and output variables. Of the four output variables that were linked to PIES, the model contains distinct deflators corresponding to XMFN29 and XRGU49 only. These two price variables—PXMFN29 and PXRGU49, respectively—were linked to PIES. The model does not contain explicit deflators corresponding to XMG11+12 and XMG13. Rather, the industrial price sector of the model treats all mining industries as a single aggregate. Since nonenergy goods account for a considerable share of total mining output, the deflator for mining, PXMG, was left endogenous and was not adjusted.

PXMFN29 and PXRGU49 are ratios of nominal gross products originating to the corresponding real gross products originating. As described above, the real gross products originating in SIC groups 29 and 49, XMFN29 and XRGU49, respectively, were linked directly to PIES production data. The linkages from PIES to PXMFN29 and PXRGU49 were completed by adjusting each nominal gross product originating in the manner described below and dividing the result by the corresponding real gross product originating. Nominal gross product originating in an industry is the difference between the value of the output that the industry produces and the value of the intermediate goods and services it purchases. This difference depends not only on output prices, but on output quantities, input prices, and input quantities. Therefore, both price and quantity forecasts from PIES were used to adjust the nominal gross products originating in SIC groups 29 and 49. In both cases, the 1975 through 1984 values of the relevant PIES prices and quantities were generated by interpolating between 1974 historical values and the corresponding 1985 PIES values at a constant compound annual rate.[k]

Nominal gross product originating in SIC group 29 was calculated as a sum of two components. One component, consisting of revenues from sales of refined petroleum, less the cost of associated inputs of crude petroleum, was computed directly from PIES data. The other component, an estimate of the remaining nominal gross product originating in SIC group 29, was obtained for

---

[k]PIES energy prices were expressed in 1975 dollars. Before 1985 PIES price projections were linked to the Wharton model, the CPI as forecast in the CONTROLLONG5/75 solution of the DRI model was used to convert them to current dollars. This forecast was the one officially adopted by the FEA for conversion purposes.

all years by subtracting the 1974 value of the first component from the 1974 control solution value of nominal gross product originating in SIC group 29.

Gross product originating in SIC group 49, in each year from 1974 through 1985, was calculated as the sum of three components: (1) the difference between revenues from utility sales of electricity and the cost of utility purchases of fossil fuels; (2) an estimate of gross product originating from the distribution of natural gas by utilities; and (3) an estimate of remaining nominal gross product originating in the group.

The first component was computed directly from PIES prices and quantities. The second component was calculated in four steps. An estimate of natural gas distributed by utilities was derived from PIES total natural gas supply data.[l] Next, an estimate of the price of gas distributed by utilities was derived from the PIES price of industrial gas in each year.[m] Then, these prices and quantities were multiplied to obtain utility revenues from sales of natural gas. Finally, an estimate of nominal gross product originating per dollar of revenues, based on 1967 input-output data, was used to transform revenues into gross product originating.[n] The third component was obtained for all years by subtracting the 1974 value of the first two components from the 1974 control solution value of nominal gross product originating in SIC group 49.

Import Quantities. In the Wharton model, import volumes are measured by constant dollar values of imports in six stage-of-processing categories. The Crude Materials, Semi-Finished Manufactures, and Finished Manufactures categories include PIES energy forms. The Wharton variables representing imports in these three categories—TMEGTCM, TMEGTMS, and TMEGTMF, respectively—were adjusted on the basis of PIES projections of physical volumes of imports of various forms of energy. Because all three categories of imports include other commodities in addition to PIES energy forms, the constant dollar value of total imports in each category was treated as a sum of the constant dollar values of imports of PIES energy forms and other commodities.

The constant dollar value of imports of individual PIES energy forms within each category was calculated from PIES projections of import quantities in three stages. First, the historical importance of each PIES energy form in its respective category was used to allocate the 1974 control solution value of imports in each category to individual PIES energy forms.[o] This allocation

---

[l]The derivation was based on the 1972 ratio of natural gas distributed by utilities to total natural gas supplies. The relevant data were obtained from [1, pp. 10, 27, and 29].

[m]The derivation was based on the 1974 ratio of the utility price of natural gas to the industrial price. These 1974 prices are in [1, p. 111].

[n]The relevant input-output data are contained in [13].

[o]The 1972 share of natural gas in the value of total imports of crude materials was obtained from [14, pp. 3 and 11]. The 1970 shares of other PIES energy forms in the value of total imports in their respective categories were taken from [8, pp. 26–27].

yielded estimates of the constant dollar value of imports of individual PIES energy forms in 1974. Second, the compound annual growth rate of imports of each PIES energy form between 1974 and 1985 was calculated using 1974 historical data and 1985 PIES projections. Third, these growth rates were applied to the corresponding 1974 estimates to obtain the constant dollar values of imports of individual PIES energy forms from 1975 through 1985.

Given the 1974 estimates of the total constant dollar value of imports of PIES energy forms within each of the three categories, the remainders of the 1974 control solution values of TMEGTCM, TMEGTMS, and TMEGTMF were assigned to imports of other commodities. From 1975 through 1985, the constant dollar value of imports of other commodities in each category was adjusted to grow at the same rate as the control solution constant dollar value of all imports in that category.

Import Prices. The Wharton model contains unit value indices for imports in each of the six stage-of-processing categories. The unit value indices corresponding to TMEGTCM, TMEGTMS, and TMEGTMF–PTMEGTCM, PTMEGTMS, and PTMEGTMF, respectively– were linked to PIES import prices and quantities.

The unit value index for imports in a particular category is equal to the ratio of the current dollar value of imports in that category to the corresponding constant dollar value. As described above, the three constant dollar values were linked to PIES import projections. The linkages to unit value indices were completed by adjusting the current dollar value of imports in each of the three categories as described below and dividing the result by the corresponding constant dollar value.

The current dollar value of imports in each stage-of-processing category was treated as a sum of the values of imports of PIES forms and other commodities. Import prices and quantities of the PIES energy forms included in each category were generated for 1974 through 1985 by interpolating between 1974 historical data and 1985 PIES projections at a constant compound annual rate. These import prices and quantities were then used to compute the total value of imports of PIES energy forms within each stage-of-processing category in each year from 1974 through 1985.

Within each category, the difference between the 1974 control solution value of all imports in the category and the 1974 total value of imports of PIES energy forms calculated above was used to estimate the value of imports of other commodities in 1974. From 1975 through 1985, the value of imports of other commodities in each category was adjusted to grow at the same compound annual rate as the control solution value of all imports in the category.

Final Demands. Because the output variables in the Wharton model could not be exogenized, the output adjustments described above provided only a partial incorporation of PIES projections of domestic energy production. In principle, with imports exogenized at levels consistent with PIES import projections, PIES projections of domestic energy production could have been fully incorporated by exogenizing final demands instead of adjusting gross products originating.

The accounting framework used on the demand side of the Wharton model precluded this alternative, however, since it divides aggregate demand into National Income Accounts (NIA) categories. These categories do not correspond well to the energy product categories used in PIES. NIA categories containing energy products typically include several other goods and services which account for a large part of the corresponding final demands.

One category of final demand in the model, real personal consumption expenditures for gasoline and oil, does include only energy products. The variable representing this category of final demand, CENG, was exogenized to reflect PIES projections of gasoline consumption. Using 1974 historical data and 1985 PIES projections, the compound annual rate of growth in total gasoline consumption between 1974 and 1985 was calculated. The value of CENG was determined in each year of the simulation period by applying this growth rate to the 1974 control solution value.

Macroeconomic Impacts

Introduction

Fourteen PIES scenarios from the 1976 *National Energy Outlook* were considered.[P] Each scenario can be regarded as a combination of a domestic energy supply and demand scenario with a hypothetical world crude oil price. Five domestic supply and demand scenarios were considered:

1. The Reference scenario makes no special assumptions concerning energy supply or demand developments. It can be regarded as a business as usual continuation of the status quo;
2. The Conservation scenario assumes a combination of business as usual domestic energy supply conditions and nonprice measures to reduce domestic energy demand;
3. The Accelerated Supply scenario assumes that business as usual demand is accompanied by measures to increase domestic energy production;
4. The Accelerated Supply and Conservation scenario assumes measures both to stimulate domestic production and to inhibit domestic consumption of energy;
5. The Supply Pessimism scenario assumes shortfalls in domestic energy production relative to business as usual supply conditions. In addition, this scenario assumes that the average price of domestic crude oil is controlled at $9 per barrel in 1975 dollars.

[P]The scenarios are described in Appendix E of [5].

Each of the first four supply and demand configurations is combined with alternative world crude oil prices of $8, $13, and $16 per barrel in 1975 dollars. The fifth supply and demand configuration is paired with alternative imported crude oil prices of $13 and $16 per barrel.

Tables 6-1 through 6-4 compare the values of selected macroeconomic variables in each energy scenario to their values in the other scenarios. The entry in a particular row and column is the difference between the value of the relevant macroeconomic variable for the scenarios designated by the row and column headings, respectively. The macroeconomic impacts of the domestic energy supply, domestic energy demand, and world crude oil price assumptions underlying the scenarios can be isolated by comparing the simulation results for scenarios which differ only with respect to each type of assumption.

Limitations

Several caveats bear on the interpretation of the simulation results. Owing to both methodological deficiencies and data unavailability, the simulation results provide only a rough gauge of the economic impacts associated with alternative energy scenarios.

It was noted in the previous methodological discussion that the output variables in the Wharton model could not be exogenized at levels consistent with PIES projections of domestic energy production, and that the accounting framework used on the demand side of the model precluded the use of final demand adjustments to incorporate those PIES projections. As a result, the simulation results did not fully reflect PIES projections of domestic energy production.

The simulation results were also affected by imprecisions in the linkages from PIES to macroeconomic variables in the Wharton model. Most of the macroeconomic variables included nonenergy components. Since forecasts of the components were not available, essentially ad hoc assumptions had to be made concerning their values. These assumptions introduced an arbitrary element into the linkages.

The precision of the linkages was further impeded by the need to generate values of the macroeconomic variables in time periods for which PIES projections were not available. Interpolation between 1974 and 1985 values of mcaroeonomic and PIES variables imposed an arbitrary growth path on the macroeconomic variables which were linked to PIES. Furthermore, it was sometimes impossible to obtain a historical output price whose definition was identical to the corresponding PIES variable.[q] This may have produced errors in the growth rates used for interpolation.

---

[q]The supply side of PIES consists of linear constraints developed on the basis of expert judgments. It was not estimated historically.

Table 6-1
Real GNP, Actual and Percent Differences between Cases, 1985 (Billions of 1958 Dollars)

Scenario		1	2	3	4	5	6	7	8	9	10	11	12	13
Reference $13	2	6.08 (0.51)												
Reference $16	3	0.83 (0.07)	-5.24 (-0.43)											
Conservation $8	4	2.87 (0.24)		2.04 (0.17)										
Conservation $13	5	5.77 (0.48)	-0.31 (-0.03)	4.93 (0.41)	2.90 (0.24)									
Conservation $16	6	7.60 (0.63)	1.53 (0.13)	6.77 (0.56)	4.73 (0.39)	1.83 (0.15)								
Accelerated Supply $8	7	18.35 (1.53)	12.28 (1.02)	17.52 (1.46)	15.48 (1.29)	12.59 (1.04)	10.75 (0.89)							
Accelerated Supply $13	8	26.10 (2.18)	20.02 (1.66)	25.26 (2.11)	23.23 (1.93)	20.33 (1.69)	18.49 (1.53)	7.74 (0.64)						
Accelerated Supply $16	9	33.71 (2.81)	27.64 (2.29)	32.88 (2.74)	30.84 (2.57)	27.94 (2.32)	26.11 (2.16)	15.36 (1.26)	7.61 (0.62)					
Accelerated Supply/Conservation $8	10	14.47 (1.21)	8.39 (0.70)	13.63 (1.14)	11.60 (0.96)	8.70 (0.72)	6.86 (0.57)	-3.89 (-0.32)	-11.63 (-0.95)	-19.24 (-1.56)				
Accelerated Supply/Conservation $13	11	19.67 (1.64)	13.60 (1.13)	18.84 (1.57)	16.80 (1.40)	13.91 (1.15)	12.07 (1.00)	1.32 (0.11)	-6.42 (-0.52)	-14.04 (-1.14)	5.21 (0.43)			
Accelerated Supply/Conservation $16	12	30.21 (2.52)	24.14 (2.00)	29.38 (2.45)	27.34 (2.27)	24.44 (2.03)	22.61 (1.87)	11.86 (0.97)	4.11 (0.34)	-3.50 (-0.28)	15.74 (1.30)	10.54 (0.86)		
Supply Pessimism $13	13	-13.45 (-1.12)	-19.52 (-1.62)	-14.28 (-1.19)	-16.32 (-1.36)	-19.22 (-1.59)	-21.05 (-1.74)	-31.80 (-2.61)	-39.55 (-3.23)	-47.16 (-3.83)	-27.91 (-2.30)	-33.12 (-2.72)	-43.66 (-3.55)	
Supply Pessimism $16	14	-21.09 (-1.76)	-27.17 (-2.25)	-21.93 (-1.83)	-23.96 (-1.99)	-26.86 (-2.23)	-28.70 (-2.38)	-39.45 (-3.24)	-47.19 (-3.85)	-54.80 (-4.45)	-35.56 (-2.93)	-40.77 (-3.35)	-51.30 (-4.17)	-7.64 (-0.64)

Source: Author's estimates.
Note: The first column shows the differences between the other scenarios and the Reference $8 scenario.

Table 6-2
Personal Consumption Expenditures, Actual and Percent Differences between Cases, 1985 (Billions of 1958 Dollars)

Scenario		1	2	3	4	5	6	7	8	9	10	11	12	13
Reference $13	2	-5.12 (-0.67)												
Reference $16	3	-10.57 (-1.39)	-5.45 (-0.72)											
Conservation $8	4	3.08 (0.40)	8.20 (1.08)	13.65 (1.82)										
Conservation $13	5	-3.39 (-0.44)	1.73 (0.23)	7.18 (0.96)	-6.47 (-0.85)									
Conservation $16	6	-6.03 (-0.79)	-0.91 (-0.12)	4.54 (0.60)	-9.11 (-1.19)	-2.64 (-0.35)								
Accelerated Supply $8	7	7.56 (0.99)	12.68 (1.68)	18.13 (2.41)	4.48 (0.59)	10.95 (1.44)	13.60 (1.80)							
Accelerated Supply $13	8	4.42 (0.58)	9.54 (1.26)	14.99 (1.99)	1.34 (0.17)	7.80 (1.03)	10.45 (1.38)	-3.15 (-0.41)						
Accelerated Supply $16	9	7.14 (0.94)	12.26 (1.62)	17.71 (2.36)	4.06 (0.53)	10.53 (1.39)	13.17 (1.74)	-0.42 (-0.05)	2.73 (0.36)					
Accelerated Supply/Conservation $8	10	7.74 (1.02)	12.86 (1.70)	18.31 (2.44)	4.66 (0.61)	11.13 (1.47)	13.77 (1.82)	0.18 (0.02)	3.32 (0.43)	0.60 (0.08)				
Accelerated Supply/Conservation $13	11	4.48 (0.59)	9.60 (1.27)	15.05 (2.00)	1.40 (0.18)	7.87 (1.04)	10.51 (1.39)	-3.08 (-0.40)	0.06 (0.01)	-2.66 (-0.35)	-3.26 (-0.42)			
Accelerated Supply/Conservation $16	12	9.26 (1.21)	14.38 (1.90)	19.83 (2.64)	6.18 (0.81)	12.64 (1.67)	15.29 (2.02)	1.69 (0.22)	4.84 (0.63)	2.11 (0.27)	1.52 (0.20)	4.78 (0.62)		
Supply Pessimism $13	13	-9.67 (-1.27)	-4.55 (-0.60)	0.90 (0.12)	-12.75 (-1.67)	-6.28 (-0.83)	-3.64 (-.48)	-17.23 (-2.24)	-14.09 (-1.84)	-16.81 (-2.19)	-17.41 (-2.26)	-14.15 (-1.85)	-18.93 (-2.45)	
Supply Pessimism $16	14	-16.14 (-2.12)	-11.02 (-1.46)	-5.57 (-0.74)	-19.22 (-2.51)	-12.75 (-1.68)	-10.11 (-1.34)	-23.88 (-3.08)	-20.55 (-2.68)	-23.38 (-3.03)	-23.88 (-3.10)	-20.62 (-2.69)	-25.39 (-3.29)	-6.47 (-0.86)

Source: Author's estimates.
Note: The first column shows the differences between the other scenarios and the Reference $8 scenario.

Table 6-3
Fixed Investment, Actual and Percent Differences betewen Cases, 1985 (Billions of 1958 Dollars)

Scenario		1	2	3	4	5	6	7	8	9	10	11	12	13
Reference $13	2	6.93 (3.06)												
Reference $16	3	5.62 (2.49)	-1.30 (-0.56)											
Conservation $8	4	-2.00 (-0.89)	-8.93 (-3.83)	-7.63 (-3.29)										
Conservation $13	5	3.29 (1.46)	-3.63 (-1.56)	-2.33 (-1.00)	5.30 (2.36)									
Conservation $16	6	6.51 (2.88)	-0.42 (-0.18)	0.88 (0.38)	8.51 (3.80)	3.21 (1.40)								
Accelerated Supply $8	7	8.81 (3.89)	1.88 (0.81)	3.18 (1.37)	10.81 (4.82)	5.51 (2.40)	2.30 (0.99)							
Accelerated Supply $13	8	14.63 (6.47)	7.70 (3.31)	9.01 (3.89)	16.63 (7.42)	11.34 (4.94)	8.12 (3.49)	5.82 (2.48)						
Accelerated Supply $16	9	18.81 (8.32)	11.90 (5.10)	13.20 (5.70)	20.83 (9.29)	15.53 (6.77)	12.32 (5.29)	10.01 (4.26)	4.19 (1.74)					
Accelerated Supply/Conseration $8	10	2.89 (1.28)	-4.04 (-1.73)	-2.73 (-1.18)	4.89 (2.18)	-0.40 (-0.18)	-3.29 (-1.55)	-5.92 (-2.52)	-11.74 (-4.88)	-15.93 (-6.50)				
Accelerated Supply/Conservetion $13	11	7.96 (3.52)	1.04 (0.45)	2.34 (1.01)	9.97 (4.45)	4.67 (2.04)	1.46 (0.63)	-0.84 (-0.36)	-6.67 (-2.77)	-10.86 (-4.43)	5.07 (2.22)			
Accelerated Supply/Conservetion $16	12	13.12 (5.80)	6.19 (2.66)	7.50 (3.23)	15.12 (6.75)	9.82 (4.28)	6.61 (2.84)	4.31 (1.84)	-1.51 (-0.63)	-5.70 (-2.33)	10.23 (4.47)	5.15 (2.20)		
Supply Pessimism $13	13	-1.62 (-0.72)	-8.55 (-3.67)	-7.24 (-3.13)	0.38 (0.17)	-4.92 (-2.14)	-8.13 (-3.49)	-10.43 (-4.44)	-16.25 (-6.75)	-20.44 (-8.35)	-4.51 (-1.97)	-9.59 (-4.09)	-14.74 (-6.16)	
Supply Pessimism $16	14	-3.47 (-1.53)	-10.40 (-4.46)	-9.09 (-3.92)	-1.47 (-0.65)	-6.77 (-2.95)	-9.98 (-4.29)	-12.28 (-5.23)	-18.10 (-7.52)	-22.29 (-9.10)	-6.36 (-2.78)	-11.44 (-4.88)	-16.59 (-6.93)	-1.85 (-0.82)

Source: Author's Estimates.
Note: The first column shows the differences between the other scenarios and the Reference $8 scenario.

Table 6-4
Net Exports, Actual and Percent Differences between Cases, 1985 (Billions of 1958 Dollars)

Scenario		1	2	3	4	5	6	7	8	9	10	11	12	13
Reference $13	2	4.01 (146.5)												
Reference $16	3	5.81 (211.9)	1.79 (26.6)											
Conservation $8	4	1.62 (59.0)	−2.40 (−35.5)	−4.19 (−49.0)										
Conservation $13	5	5.56 (203.1)	1.55 (23.0)	−0.24 (−2.8)	3.95 (90.6)									
Conservation $16	6	6.97 (254.5)	2.96 (43.8)	1.17 (13.7)	5.35 (122.9)	1.41 (16.9)								
Accelerated Supply $8	7	1.26 (46.1)	−2.75 (−40.7)	−4.54 (−53.2)	−0.36 (−8.2)	−4.30 (−51.8)	−5.71 (−58.8)							
Accelerated Supply $13	8	6.08 (221.9)	2.07 (30.6)	0.27 (3.2)	4.46 (102.5)	0.52 (6.2)	−0.89 (−9.2)	4.82 (120.4)						
Accelerated Supply $16	9	6.52 (238.0)	2.51 (37.2)	0.72 (8.4)	4.50 (122.6)	0.96 (11.5)	−0.45 (−4.6)	5.26 (131.4)	0.44 (5.0)					
Accelerated Supply/Conservation $8	10	3.24 (118.1)	−0.78 (−11.5)	−2.57 (−30.1)	1.62 (37.2)	−2.33 (−28.0)	−3.73 (−38.5)	1.98 (49.4)	−2.84 (−32.2)	−3.28 (−35.5)				
Accelerated Supply/Conservation $13	11	6.53 (238.2)	2.51 (37.2)	0.72 (8.4)	4.91 (112.7)	0.96 (11.6)	−0.45 (−4.6)	5.26 (131.6)	0.45 (5.1)	0.01 (0.1)	3.29 (55.0)			
Accelerated Supply/Conservation $16	12	6.79 (247.7)	2.77 (41.1)	1.98 (11.5)	5.17 (118.7)	1.22 (14.7)	−0.18 (−1.9)	5.53 (138.1)	0.71 (8.0)	0.27 (2.9)	3.55 (59.4)	0.26 (2.8)		
Supply Pessimism $13	13	−1.77 (−64.8)	−5.79 (−85.7)	−7.58 (−88.7)	−33.9 (−77.9)	−7.34 (−88.4)	−8.75 (−90.1)	−3.04 (−75.9)	−7.86 (−89.1)	−8.30 (−89.6)	−5.01 (−83.9)	−8.30 (−89.6)	−8.56 (−90.0)	
Supply Pessimism $16	14	−0.80 (−29.2)	−4.81 (−71.3)	−6.60 (−77.3)	−2.42 (−55.5)	−6.36 (−76.6)	−7.77 (−80.0)	−2.06 (−51.5)	−6.88 (−78.0)	−7.32 (−79.1)	−4.04 (−67.5)	−7.33 (−79.1)	−7.59 (−79.6)	0.98 (101.1)

Source: Author's estimates.
Note: The first column shows the differences between the other scenarios and the Reference $8 scenario.

The above problems may have produced serious bias in the levels of the simulation results and, at the least, suggest that the simulations of particular PIES scenarios not be treated as economic forecasts. They can be expected to have had a less serious effect on the differences between simulations, however, because they would have tended to bias the simulations of different scenarios in a similar fashion.

A more serious deficiency, affecting both the PIES and macroeconomic simulations, is the potential inconsistency between the macroeconomic forecast used to drive PIES and the macroeconomic simulation results based on PIES output. Changes in general economic activity imply changes in the energy sector, and vice versa. Different PIES scenarios imply different levels of the macroeconomic variables in the PIES model, but the same macroeconomic forecast was used for all PIES scenarios. This inconsistency may have produced errors both in the levels of the simulation results and in the differences between simulations.

Price Impacts

Within the $8 to $16 range considered, higher world crude oil prices generally have a small positive impact on real output for given energy supply and demand scenarios. This impact reflects increases in domestic energy production and reductions in imports projected by PIES.

If crude oil is imported and domestic energy prices are market determined, the domestically produced crude oil price equals the world crude oil price. Hence, increases in the world crude oil price raise domestic energy prices and stimulate production and capital formation in domestic energy-producing industries. As a result of the structure of the financial sector in the Wharton model, the money supply expands to accommodate the increased energy related investment, leaving interest rates virtually unchanged. Consequently, investment increases in energy-producing sectors without crowding out investment in other sectors. The result is an increase in total real investment expenditures.

In most instances, reductions in real personal consumption expenditures resulting from higher energy prices partially offset the increases in real investment and net exports. Real personal consumption expenditures for nondurables decline as a result of decreases in gasoline and oil consumption and the negative impact that higher prices have on real income. Real personal consumption expenditures for durables and services also decline as a result of the adverse impact on real personal income. In all cases, higher world crude oil prices result in a higher domestic price level as measured by the GNP implicit price deflator.

Conservation Impacts

Energy conservation measures reduce the demand for energy at given energy prices. With domestic supply conditions and the world crude oil price given, such a reduction in energy demand lowers energy prices, production, and imports. These energy sector changes generally have a favorable impact on personal consumption expenditures, the GNP implicit price deflator, and net exports. Since these changes have a negative impact on investment, however, the effect of conservation on real GNP is small in magnitude and indeterminate in sign.

Owing to the positive impact that lower energy prices associated with conservation have on consume purchasing power, a decline in real personal consumption expenditures for gasoline and oil is more than offset by increases in other real personal consumption expenditures. The result is an increase in total real personal consumption expenditures. At the same time, lower energy prices and production reduce real investment expenditures in energy-producing industries. Given the stability of interest rates in the Wharton model, these reductions are not offset by gains in other sectors. Consequently, conservation results in a decline in total real investment expenditures.

Relative to the Reference scenario at a given world crude oil price, personal consumption expenditure and net export gains outweigh the investment decline in the Conservation scenario and increase real GNP slightly. Compared to the Accelerated Supply scenario at a given world oil price, the investment decline outweights personal consumption expenditure and net export gains in the Accelerated Supply and Conservation scenario and reduces real GNP slightly.

Domestic Supply Impacts

With demand conditions and the world crude oil price given, acceleration of domestic energy production exerts a positive influence on real economic activity. In every instance, accelerated supply has a favorable impact on real net exports, reflecting decreases in energy imports. Furthermore, both real consumption and investment expenditures are always higher in the accelerated supply scenarios than in the corresponding business as usual supply scenarios.

Acceleration of domestic energy production has a pronounced impact on total real investment expenditures. Increases in energy production have direct positive impacts on investment in energy-producing industries. Since endogenous monetary expansion prevents offsetting investment declines in other industries, acceleration of domestic energy production increases total real investment.

Higher levels of real investment and lower energy imports have a favorable effect on employment and real personal income. In response to the gains in employment and personal income, real personal consumption expenditures are also higher under conditions of accelerated supply.

The impact of accelerated energy production on the overall domestic price level varies with the world crude oil price. As the world crude oil price rises, substitution of domestically produced energy for imported petroleum has an increasingly favorable impact on the GNP implicit price deflator.

Compared to the results for the corresponding scenarios with business as usual supply conditions, the results for the Supply Pessimism scenarios indicate that the combination of significant shortfalls in domestic fossil fuel production and the continuation of price controls on domestically produced energy adversely affects real GNP and all of its major components. These impacts are directly opposite to the favorable impacts of accelerated energy supply. Although the price controls included in the pessimistic supply scenarios may soften the impacts of adverse supply developments on energy consumers, they also further inhibit energy production and investment. It is impossible to say whether the negative economic impacts of the pessimistic supply scenarios would be larger or smaller without price controls.

Conclusions

The Wharton model is essentially a long-run model. It effectively minimizes frictions that may be important in the short run, but become irrelevant over time as the economy responds to a given disturbance and approaches a new long-run growth path. In the simulations reported here, the minimization is effected through endogenous adjustments set in motion by changes originating in the energy sector. Endogenous change in the quantity of money that exerts a stabilizing influence on total investment is one such adjustment. Another is endogenous price-sensitive substitution among the outputs of the various producing sectors: as energy prices increase or decrease, the consumption of energy required to meet a given level of final demand decreases or increases, respectively. Although these adjustments do not correspond to short-run responses that actually occur to changes in the energy sector, they enhance the ability of the Wharton model to capture the long-run impacts of such changes. Consequently, the simulated impacts of each type of energy assumption should agree with expectations based on long-run theoretical considerations.

The simulations indicate that increases in the world crude oil price need not have an adverse long-run impact on real GNP, but do reduce real personal consumption expenditures. Theoretical considerations tend to support this finding. Since the demand for imported crude oil is inelastic, an increase in the world crude price increases expenditures for imported oil. In the long run, following adjustments in international markets, increased expenditures on imported oil induce an expansion in real export demand. Increases in world oil prices also stimulate domestic energy production and related investment. As a result of the increases in export demand and domestic energy production, higher world oil prices may have a positive long-run impact on real GNP. However, a larger share of domestic output must be exported to pay for imported oil, thereby reducing domestic living standards.

Judging by the simulation results, energy conservation appears to have no significant long-run impact on real GNP or its major components. This finding may reflect theoretical ambiguities concerning the economic impact of energy conservation. Although energy conservation reduces both expenditures for imported oil and the vulnerability of the domestic economy to disruptions in foreign oil supplies, its implications for economic growth are unclear. Efficient energy conservation measures—that is, those whose energy-saving benefits outweigh their costs—reduce costs for a given level of output and induce an expansion in real GNP. Energy conservation measures that are efficient in this sense would be undertaken voluntarily, given adequate information concerning their energy-saving potential. However, legally mandated conservation measures can have a negative impact on economic growth. For example, mandated investments in expensive energy-conserving technologies that would not be undertaken at market determined domestic energy prices are less productive than the alternatives they replace.

Of the three types of energy sector assumptions examined here, the simulations of changes in domestic energy supply conditions provide the most conclusive empirical results. The favorable economic impacts of increases—and, conversely, the negative impacts of decreases—in domestic energy supplies are fully consistent with *a priori* expectations. Relative to business as usual supply conditions, accelerated supply conditions increase energy supplies at given energy prices. With the exception of crude oil, whose domestic price is governed by the world price, such increases in domestic energy supplies reduce energy prices for a given level of demand. At the quantity demanded responds to the supply-induced decline in energy prices, real output of the economy expands. Furthermore, to the extent that domestic energy sources whose prices become lower can be substituted for crude oil, expenditures for imports of crude oil are reduced. Similar increases in the supply of domestic crude oil directly reduce expenditures for imported oil and, *pari passu*, generate long-run increases in real personal consumption expenditures. Conversely, pessimistic domestic supply conditions reduce domestic energy supplies at given prices and induce a contraction in real output and consumption.

References

1. American Gas Association. Department of Statistics, *1974 Gas Facts* (Arlington, Va.: American Gas Association, 1975).

2. Askin, A. Bradley. "The Macroeconomic Implications of Alternative Energy Scenarios." In Askin and Kraft, eds., *Econometric Dimensions of Energy Demand and Supply* (Lexington, Mass.: D.C. Health and Company, 1976), pp. 91–109.

3. Executive Office of the President, Office of Management and Budget. *1972 Standard Industrial Classification Manual* (Washington, D.C.: U.S. Government Printing Office).

4. Federal Energy Administration. *Monthly Energy Review* (February 1976).

5. Federal Energy Administration. *1976 National Energy Outlook* (Washington, D.C.: U.S. Government Printing Office, 1976).

6. Federal Energy Administration. *Project Independence Report* (Washington, D.C.: U.S. Government Printing Office, 1974).

7. Preston, Ross S. *The Wharton Annual and Industry Forecasting Model* (Philadelphia, Pa.: University of Pennsylvania, 1972).

8. U.S. Department of Commerce, Bureau of the Census. *Indexes of U.S. Exports and Imports by Economic Class: 1919-1971* (Washington, D.C.: U.S. Government Printing Office, 1972).

9. U.S. Department of Commerce, Bureau of the Census. "Industry Series: Natural Gas Liquids." *1972 Census of Mineral Industries* (Washington, D.C.: U.S. Government Printing Office, 1975).

10. U.S. Department of Commerce, Bureau of the Census. "Industry Series: Oil and Gas Field Operations." *1972 Census of Mineral Industries* (Washington, D.C.: U.S. Government Printing Office, 1975).

11. U.S. Department of Commerce, Bureau of the Census. "Industry Series: Oil and Gas Field Services." *1972 Census of Mineral Industries* (Washington, D.C.: U.S. Government Printing Office, 1975).

12. U.S. Department of Commerce, Bureau of the Census. "Industry Series: Petroleum and Coal Products." *1972 Census of Manufactures* (Washington, D.C.: U.S. Government Printing Office, 1975).

13. U.S. Department of Commerce, Bureau of Economic Analysis. *Input-Output Structure of the U.S. Economy: 1967*, vol. 2 (Washington, D.C.: U.S. Government Printing Office, 1974).

14. U.S. Department of Commerce, Domestic and International Business Administration. "United States Foreign Trade, Annual, 1968-1974." *Overseas Business Reports* (Washington, D.C.: U.S. Government Printing Office, 1975).

15. Wharton Econometric Forecasting Associates. "Annual and Industry Model Equations." (June 1975).

7

Macroeconomic Simulations of Alternative Energy Scenarios with the DRI Model
Richard L. Farman and Gerard L. Lagace

Introduction

The future macroeconomic environment of the United States will depend in part on developments in the energy sector of the economy. Some of these developments will reflect usual market forces; others will result from the implementation of specific government policies and decisions of foreign oil producing countries. Because of the uncertainty attached to any particular course of energy development, assessment of the future macroeconomic environment must encompass a range of energy scenarios.

Ascertaining the macroeconomic implications of energy scenarios presents several difficulties. Specific energy sector developments impact on the economy and are, in turn, then affected themselves. Although such feedback effects between the general economy and the energy sector may be significant, little work has been done to construct models that recognize both sources of interactions.[a] Most macroeconometric models are final demand oriented. Models with an explicit supply sector typically aggregate energy and nonenergy variables, do not allow for input substitution possibilities between energy and nonenergy inputs, or both.

This chapter analyzes the effects that alternative energy developments are likely to have on the U.S. economy in 1985. We examine thirteen energy scenarios that differ with respect to assumptions concerning the price of imported oil and domestic energy demand and supply conditions. The analysis assumes that federal authorities take no fiscal or monetary actions to offset the impacts reported, although many of the impacts could be reduced or eliminated through such actions.[b] The sections that follow describe the methodology, its limitations, and the empirical findings of the analysis.

Methodology

Macroeconomic forecasts consistent with the thirteen energy scenarios were estimated by incorporating information about them generated with the Project

---

[a]A notable exception is the Hudson-Jorgenson model, described in [3].

[b]Such policies are conjectural, and focusing on them would show the effects of energy developments and aggregate demand management policies in combination rather than the effects of energy developments alone.

Independence Evaluation System (PIES) into the Data Resources, Inc. Quarterly Econometric Model of the U.S. Economy (DRI) model and then simulating the effects on the economy.

PIES consists of an econometric demand model, linear constraint supply models, and a fixed-point programming integrating framework. It was constructed to simulate energy scenarios encompassing a variety of assumptions concerning technology, resource availability, domestic energy policy, and the like. The demand model determines the quantity of energy demanded as a function of energy prices and other variables. Among the principal exogenous variables driving the demand model are macroeconomic variables taken from a forecast of the economy. The supply models represent energy production possibilities as a set of linear constraints. The integrating framework solves for equilibrium prices and quantities given demand model price elasticities and supply model constraints. PIES information on the prices, consumption, domestic production, and imports of various energy forms served as input to the macroeconomic analysis presented in this chapter.[c]

Alternative simulations of the U.S. economy corresponding to the thirteen energy scenarios were generated with the 1975 version of the DRI model. The economy was simulated for each scenario by modifying the assumptions underlying a standard solution of the DRI model and then resolving the DRI model. CONTROLLONG5/75, reflecting DRI's most likely long-term forecast of the economy as of May 1975, was adopted as the standard solution, because its values for certain variables were used as inputs to the PIES energy simulations. The alternative simulations of the economy were then compared to determine the macroeconomic effects of the energy scenarios.

PIES information was transformed into the appropriate form and substituted into the DRI model at six entry points. Two of the entry points were in the domestic sector: the WPI for fuels and related products and power (WPI05NS) and personal consumption expenditures on gasoline and oil in 1958 dollars (CNGAS58). Four of the entry points were in the foreign sector: the constant dollar value of crude oil imports (IMPCRUDEOIL67); the constant dollar value of refined petroleum product imports (IMPREFINEDOIL67); the average unit value index for crude oil imports (JMPCROILNS); and the average unit value index for refined petroleum product imports (JMPREFINEDNS).

The DRI model is highly sensitive to changes in WPI05NS, as that price index directly or indirectly affects virtually all wholesale, consumer, and final demand price indexes in the model. A six-step procedure was used to exogenize WPI05NS at levels consistent with the energy prices generated by PIES. First, 1967 and 1974 historical price data on eight different energy products covered

---

[c]PIES is described in the technical appendixes of both [1] and [2].

by WPIO5NS were obtained.[d] Second, the 1974 prices were converted to index numbers with 1967 as the base: that is, 1967 = 1.0. Third, PIES 1985 prices for the same eight energy categories in 1975 constant dollar prices were transformed into current dollar prices by multiplying them by the ratio of the 1985 and 1975 CPI values found in CONTROLLONG5/75. Fourth, the resulting 1985 current dollar prices were converted into index numbers with 1967 as a base year by dividing them by the 1967 historical prices found in step one. Fifth, quarterly price index values were generated for each year between 1974 and 1985 for all eight forms of energy by interpolating between the annual index values for 1974 and 1985 at a constant growth rate. Finally, quarterly values for WPIO5NS were constructed as a weighted average of the quarterly price indexes, using weights published by the Bureau of Labor Statistics (BLS).

CNGAS58 was constrained to be consistent with the total demand for gasoline as forecasted by PIES. First, the 78 percent of gasoline estimated from input-output data to be historically sold to consumers was used to convert the total gasoline usage reported by PIES into a consumer usage. Second, this consumer usage was multiplied by the 1985 price of gasoline to estimate personal consumption expenditures on gasoline and oil in 1985. Third, the same interpolation routine applied to WPIO5NS was applied to the known CNGAS58 value for 1974 and the estimated value for 1985 to derive quarterly values.

JMPCROILNS and JMPREFINEDNS were exogenously set at levels consistent with the 1985 prices forecasted by PIES for these two categories of imports. Similarly, IMPCRUDEOIL67 and IMPREFINEDOIL67 were set at levels consistent with PIES forecasts of 1985 import volumes for crude oil and refined petroleum products. Quarterly values for 1974 through 1985 for all four variables were derived with the constant growth rate interpolation routine used for WPIO5NS.

Limitations

Methodological Limitations

The analysis presented in this chapter is subject to some methodological limitations. The principal ones are the absence of feedback effects between the energy and macroeconometric models used, the absence of a detailed supply sector in the macroeconometric model, inadequate treatment of energy investment, and the use of highly aggregated energy data in the DRI model.

---

[d]The eight energy products, together with their 1967 and 1974 prices, are: crude oil, $6.55 and $13.09 per barrel; residual oil, $2.29 and $11.11 per barrel; distillate oil, $4.05 and $10.61 per barrel; gasoline, $5.91 and $11.14 per barrel; other refined products, $3.97 and $10.80 per barrel; natural gas, $0.71 and $1.10 per 1000 cubic feet; coal, $4.62 and $15.72 per short ton; electricity, $13.83 and $21.26 per 1000 kilowatt hours.

Ideally, the DRI model and PIES should be solved simultaneously or in iterative fashion to allow for feedback effects, since each uses output from the other. Successive iterations to take such feedback effects into account were not made, however.

The DRI model does not have a detailed supply sector. Therefore, it is not feasible to constrain domestic energy supplies to the levels generated by PIES. Moreover, with one exception, the domestic sector of the model does not contain energy specific final demand variables which can be constrained to be consistent with PIES demand quantities. The exception is CNGAS58, constrained to be consistent with PIES as explained earlier.

The DRI model treats price changes as if induced by supply shifts, that is, movements along demand curves. However, conservation features of some scenarios imply demand shifts. Since demand and supply shifts resulting in the same price effect have opposite effects on output, the DRI model misrepresents the effects of energy conservation. The consequences of misrepresenting energy demand shifts as energy supply shifts are not as serious when oil is imported, which is the usual case, as when no oil is imported. Figure 7-1 illustrates the former situation. S is the domestic supply curve for oil. Similarly, D_1 and D_2 represent two different demand curves for oil. Given a world oil price of P_1, the portion of the domestic supply curve above P_1 is irrelevant since quantities demanded in excess of Q_1 are imported. The price of oil and the volume of domestic oil remain unchanged at P_1 and Q_1, respectively, after conservation reduces domestic oil demand from D_1 to D_2. Both the demand for oil and imports of oil decrease by $Q_2 Q_3$. Thus, the effects of energy conservation can be captured in the DRI model by reducing oil imports. Only when domestic oil demand falls below Q_1, the point of zero imports, does a shift occur which cannot be represented.

Changes in domestic energy production imply changes in energy investment. The investment assumptions underlying CONTROLLONG5/75 were not altered to reflect such expenditures, because data to do so were not available. The only investment changes that occur are those generated by changes in general macroeconomic conditions.

WPI05NS is the sole domestic energy price variable in the DRI model, except for a deflator for consumption expenditures on gasoline and motor oil. Computed as a weighted average index of PIES energy prices, it treats these prices as simple scalars of one another. Consequently, it does not recognize the differential impacts associated with changes in the various individual prices.

The only foreign sector energy prices and volumes changed were those for imported crude, distillate, and residual oil, since no other foreign sector energy variables appear in the DRI model. Consequently, the impacts of changes in the foreign sector are understated to some extent.

Data Problems

The analysis suffers from several data problems. Historical energy prices for 1967 and 1974 consistent with PIES energy prices for 1985 are not available.

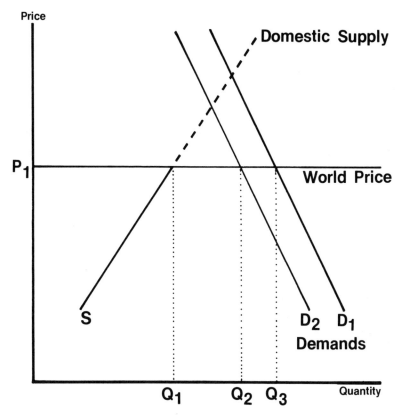

Figure 7.1. The Effects of a Shift in the Demand for Oil when Oil is Imported

Not all energy prices are defined the same way or measured at the same stage of production and distribution in PIES and the DRI model. Interpolating between 1974 and 1985 to generate quarterly data for all intervening years produces arbitrary simulation results for 1985 owing to the important role lags play in the DRI model.

The prices of imported distillate and residual oil in 1985 were not available from PIES for one scenario where no oil was imported. The 1985 prices from another related scenario were used to estimate the 1975-1985 values of distillate and residual oil imports for the affected scenario.

Macroeconomic Impacts

Introduction

As pointed out in the introduction, the thirteen energy scenarios considered differ with respect to their assumptions concerning the price of imported oil and domestic energy demand and supply conditions. Three alternative prices of imported oil are considered: $8, $13, and $16 per barrel in 1975 dollars. Five alternative sets of assumptions about domestic energy conditions are considered.

The Reference scenarios assume continuation of a business as usual situation through 1985 with no special energy demand or supply developments. The Conservation scenarios posit implementation of nonprice measures to conserve energy. The Accelerated Supply scenarios assume that policies to increase domestic energy supplies are adopted, but that business as usual demand conditions are retained. The Accelerated Supply and Conservation scenarios assume that policies both to increase domestic energy supplies and to reduce energy demand are implemented. The Supply Pessimism scenarios assume that domestic energy production is constrained by a ceiling price of $9 per barrel in 1975 dollars on domestic crude oil, unfavorable oil discovery rates, slower leasing of outer continental shelf acreage, and reduced Alaskan North Slope oil production in the 1980s.[e]

Tables 7-1 through 7-5 summarize the macroeconomic simulation results for the thirteen energy scenarios. Each entry in a table reports the value of a selected economic variable for the scenario designated by the row heading relative to its value for the scenario designated by the column heading. The economic implications of a particular assumption can be ascertained by comparing those scenarios that differ only with respect to that assumption.

Imported Crude Oil Prices[f]

With only one exception, higher imported crude oil prices adversely affect the economy, *ceterus paribus*. The general price level rises as higher foreign crude oil prices push up the average price of energy consumed domestically. This rise induces an unfavorable real balance effect which reduces real aggregate demand.

The 1985 macroeconomic implications of higher imported crude oil prices are considerable. On average, raising the price of imported crude oil from $8 to $13 for given energy supply and demand conditions increases the GNP implicit price deflator by 6.9 percent. Similarly, raising the price of imported crude oil from $13 to $16 increases the general price level by 2.4 percent. In

---

[e]The DRI model solution algorithm did not converge for the Accelerated Supply $16 scenario. The Supply Pessimism $8 scenario was not considered, because the $9 ceiling price on domestic crude oil would be redundant in that situation. Detailed descriptions of the scenarios are available in Appendix E of [1].

[f]The implications of different imported crude oil prices can be seen by comparing the scenarios for each set of domestic energy demand and supply conditions among themselves at the different imported crude oil prices.

Table 7-1
Percent Differences in the 1985 GNP Implicit Price Deflator between Scenarios

	Case	1	2	3	4	5	6	7	8	9	10	11	12
Reference $13	2	5.9											
Reference $16	3	9.4	3.3										
Conservation $8	4	-0.5	-6.0	-9.1									
Conservation $13	5	6.2	0.3	-3.0	6.7								
Conservation $16	6	11.0	4.9	1.5	11.6	4.6							
Accelerated Supply $8	7	0.6	-5.0	-8.1	1.1	-5.3	-9.4						
Accelerated Supply $13	8	7.9	1.9	-1.4	8.4	1.6	-2.9	7.2					
Accelerated Supply/Conservation $8	9	0.2	5.4	-8.4	0.7	-5.6	-9.8	-0.4	-7.1				
Accelerated Supply/Conservation $13	10	8.0	2.0	-1.3	8.6	1.7	-2.8	7.4	0.1	7.8			
Accelerated Supply/Conservation $16	11	8.8	2.8	-0.6	9.4	2.5	-2.0	8.2	0.9	8.6	0.7		
Supply Pessimism $13	12	1.8	-3.8	-6.9	2.3	-4.1	-8.3	1.2	-5.6	1.6	-5.7	-6.4	
Supply Pessimism $16	13	2.6	-3.1	-6.2	3.1	-3.4	-7.6	2.0	-4.9	2.4	-5.0	-5.7	0.8

Source: Authors' estimates.
Note: Column 1 reports impacts for other scenarios relative to the Reference $8 scenario.

Table 7-2
Differences in 1985 Real GNP in Billions of 1958 Dollars between Scenarios (Percent Differences in Parenthesis)

	Case	1	2	3	4	5	6	7	8	9	10	11	12
Reference $13	2	-38.7 (-3.2)											
Reference $16	3	-60.6 (-5.0)	-21.9 (-1.9)										
Conservation $8	4	6.1 (0.5)	44.8 (3.8)	66.7 (5.7)									
Conservation $13	5	-36.9 (-3.0)	1.8 (0.2)	23.7 (2.0)	-43.0 (-3.5)								
Conservation $16	6	-57.2 (-4.7)	-18.5 (-1.6)	3.4 (0.3)	-63.3 (-5.2)	-20.3 (-1.7)							
Accelerated Supply $8	7	8.2 (0.7)	47.0 (4.0)	68.9 (5.9)	2.2 (0.2)	45.2 (3.8)	65.5 (5.6)						
Accelerated Supply $13	8	-29.8 (-2.4)	9.0 (0.8)	30.9 (2.7)	-35.8 (-2.9)	7.2 (0.6)	27.5 (2.4)	-38.0 (-3.1)					
Accelerated Supply/Conservation $8	9	11.0 (0.9)	49.8 (4.2)	71.6 (6.2)	4.9 (0.4)	47.9 (4.1)	68.2 (5.9)	2.8 (0.2)	40.8 (3.4)				
Accelerated Supply/Conservation $13	10	-34.4 (-2.8)	4.4 (0.4)	26.2 (2.3)	-40.5 (-3.3)	2.6 (0.2)	22.9 (2.0)	-42.6 (-3.5)	-4.6 (-0.4)	-45.4 (-3.7)			
Accelerated Supply/Conservation $16	11	-30.1 (-2.5)	8.7 (0.7)	30.5 (2.6)	-36.2 (-3.0)	6.8 (0.6)	27.1 (2.3)	-38.3 (-3.1)	-0.3 (0.0)	-41.1 (-3.3)	4.3 (0.4)		
Supply Pessimism $13	12	-37.4 (-3.1)	1.3 (0.1)	23.2 (2.0)	-43.5 (-3.6)	-0.5 (0.0)	19.8 (1.7)	-45.6 (-3.7)	-7.6 (-0.6)	-48.4 (-3.9)	-3.0 (-0.3)	-7.3 (-0.6)	
Supply Pessimism $16	13	-51.7 (-4.2)	-13.0 (-1.1)	8.9 (0.8)	-57.8 (-4.7)	-14.8 (-1.3)	5.5 (0.5)	-60.0 (-4.9)	-22.0 (-1.9)	-62.8 (-5.1)	-17.4 (-1.5)	-21.7 (-1.8)	-14.3 (-1.2)

Source: Authors' estimates.

Note: Column 1 reports impacts for other scenarios relative to the Reference $8 scenario.

Table 7-3

Differences in 1985 Personal Consumption Expenditures in Billions of 1958 Dollars between Scenarios (Percent Differences in Parenthesis)

	Case	1	2	3	4	5	6	7	8	9	10	11	12
Reference $13	2	-17.8 (-2.2)											
Reference $16	3	-26.0 (-3.2)	-8.2 (-1.0)										
Conservation $8	4	-0.4 (-0.1)	17.5 (2.2)	25.6 (3.3)									
Conservation $13	5	-18.7 (-2.3)	-0.9 (-0.1)	7.3 (0.9)	-18.4 (-2.3)								
Conservation $16	6	-23.0 (-2.9)	-5.2 (-0.7)	3.0 (0.4)	-22.6 (-2.8)	-4.3 (-0.5)							
Accelerated Supply $8	7	4.4 (0.6)	22.3 (2.8)	30.4 (3.9)	4.8 (0.6)	23.2 (2.9)	27.4 (3.5)						
Accelerated Supply $13	8	-10.4 (-1.3)	7.4 (0.9)	15.6 (2.0)	-10.0 (-1.2)	8.3 (1.1)	12.6 (1.6)	-14.9 (-1.8)					
Accelerated Supply/Conservation $8	9	1.9 (0.2)	19.7 (2.5)	27.9 (3.6)	2.3 (0.3)	20.6 (2.6)	24.9 (3.2)	-2.6 (-0.3)	12.3 (1.5)				
Accelerated Supply/Conservation $13	10	-14.2 (-1.8)	3.6 (0.5)	11.8 (1.5)	-13.8 (-1.7)	4.5 (0.6)	8.8 (1.1)	-18.7 (-2.3)	-3.8 (-0.5)	-16.1 (-2.0)			
Accelerated Supply/Conservation $16	11	-10.7 (-1.3)	7.1 (0.9)	15.3 (2.0)	-10.3 (-1.3)	8.0 (1.0)	12.3 (1.6)	-15.1 (-1.9)	-0.3 (0.0)	-12.6 (-1.6)	3.5 (0.5)		
Supply Pessimism $13	12	-20.2 (-2.5)	-2.3 (-0.3)	5.8 (0.8)	-19.8 (-2.5)	-1.4 (-0.2)	2.8 (0.4)	-24.6 (-3.0)	-9.7 (-1.2)	-22.0 (-2.7)	-5.9 (-0.8)	-9.5 (-1.2)	
Supply Pessimism $16	13	-27.5 (-3.4)	-9.7 (-1.2)	-1.5 (-0.2)	-27.1 (-3.4)	-8.8 (-1.1)	-4.5 (-0.6)	-32.0 (-3.9)	-17.1 (-2.1)	-29.4 (-3.6)	-13.3 (-1.7)	-16.8 (-2.1)	-7.4 (-0.9)

Source: Authors' estimates.

Note: Column 1 reports impacts for other scenarios relative ot the Reference $8 scenario.

Table 7-4

Differences in 1985 Gross Domestic Private Investment in Billions of 1958 Dollars between Scenarios (Percent Differences in Parenthesis)

	Case	1	2	3	4	5	6	7	8	9	10	11	12
Reference $13	2	-19.0 (-10.3)											
Reference $16	3	-27.2 (-14.7)	-8.2 (-5.0)										
Conservation $8	4	2.1 (1.1)	21.0 (21.7)	29.0 (18.6)									
Conservation $13	5	-19.5 (-10.5)	-0.5 (-0.3)	7.7 (4.9)	-21.5 (-11.5)								
Conservation $16	6	-30.6 (-16.5)	-11.6 (-7.0)	-3.4 (-2.1)	-32.6 (-17.5)	-11.1 (-6.7)							
Accelerated Supply $8	7	-0.8 (-0.5)	18.1 (10.9)	26.4 (16.7)	-2.9 (-1.5)	18.6 (11.3)	29.7 (19.3)						
Accelerated Supply $13	8	-20.0 (-10.8)	-1.0 (-0.6)	7.2 (4.6)	-22.1 (-11.8)	-0.5 (-0.3)	10.6 (6.9)	-19.2 (-10.4)					
Accelerated Supply/Conservation $8	9	0.6 (0.3)	19.6 (11.8)	27.8 (17.7)	-1.4 (-0.8)	20.1 (12.2)	31.2 (20.2)	1.5 (0.8)	20.6 (12.5)				
Accelerated Supply/Conservation $13	10	-20.9 (-11.3)	-2.0 (-1.2)	6.3 (4.0)	-23.0 (-12.3)	-1.5 (-0.9)	9.6 (6.3)	-20.1 (-10.9)	-0.9 (-0.6)	-21.6 (-11.6)			
Accelerated Supply/Conservation $16	11	-21.6 (-11.7)	-2.6 (-1.6)	5.6 (3.6)	-23.7 (-12.7)	-2.1 (-1.3)	9.0 (5.8)	-20.8 (-11.3)	-1.6 (-1.0)	-22.2 (-12.0)	-0.7 (-0.4)		
Supply Pessimism $13	12	-9.4 (-5.1)	9.6 (5.8)	17.8 (11.3)	-11.4 (-6.1)	10.1 (6.1)	21.2 (13.7)	-8.6 (-4.7)	10.6 (6.4)	-10.0 (-5.4)	11.5 (7.0)	12.2 (7.5)	
Supply Pessimism $16	13	-13.0 (-7.0)	6.0 (3.6)	14.2 (9.0)	-15.0 (-8.0)	6.5 (3.9)	17.6 (11.4)	-12.1 (-6.6)	7.0 (4.3)	-13.6 (-7.3)	8.0 (4.9)	8.6 (5.3)	-3.6 (-2.0)

Source: Authors' estimates.

Note: Column 1 reports impacts for other scenarios relative to the Reference $8 scenario.

Table 7-5
Differences in 1985 Net Exports in Billions of 1958 Dollars between Scenarios (Percent Differences in Parenthesis)

	Case	1	2	3	4	5	6	7	8	9	10	11	12
Reference $13	2	1.3 (7.8)											
Reference $16	3	1.0 (6.1)	-0.3 (-1.6)										
Conservation $8	4	4.0 (23.2)	2.6 (14.3)	2.9 (16.1)									
Conservation $13	5	4.7 (27.1)	3.3 (17.9)	3.6 (19.8)	0.7 (3.2)								
Conservation $16	6	4.3 (25.2)	3.0 (16.1)	3.3 (18.0)	0.4 (1.6)	-0.3 (-1.5)							
Accelerated Supply $8	7	3.9 (22.5)	2.5 (13.7)	2.8 (15.5)	-0.1 (-0.5)	-0.8 (-3.6)	-0.5 (-2.1)						
Accelerated Supply $13	8	6.8 (39.3)	5.4 (29.3)	5.7 (31.3)	2.8 (13.1)	2.1 (9.6)	2.4 (11.3)	2.9 (13.7)					
Accelerated Supply/Conservation $8	9	7.7 (44.9)	6.4 (34.4)	6.7 (36.6)	3.7 (17.6)	3.1 (14.0)	3.4 (15.8)	3.8 (18.3)	1.0 (4.0)				
Accelerated Supply/Conservation $13	10	7.4 (43.2)	6.1 (32.9)	6.4 (35.0)	3.4 (16.2)	2.8 (12.7)	3.1 (14.4)	3.6 (16.9)	0.7 (2.8)	-0.3 (-1.2)			
Accelerated Supply/Conservation $16	11	8.2 (47.8)	6.9 (37.1)	7.2 (39.3)	4.2 (20.0)	3.6 (16.3)	3.9 (18.1)	4.3 (20.6)	1.5 (6.1)	0.5 (2.0)	0.8 (3.2)		
Supply Pessimism $13	12	-4.4 (-25.8)	-5.8 (-31.1)	-5.5 (-30.0)	-8.4 (-39.7)	-9.1 (-41.6)	-8.8 (-40.7)	-8.3 (-39.4)	-11.2 (-46.7)	-12.1 (-48.8)	-11.9 (-48.2)	-12.6 (-49.8)	
Supply Pessimism $16	13	-6.5 (-38.1)	-7.9 (-42.5)	-7.6 (-41.6)	-10.5 (-49.7)	-11.2 (-51.3)	-10.9 (-50.5)	-10.4 (-49.4)	-13.3 (-55.5)	-14.3 (-57.3)	-14.0 (-56.7)	-14.7 (-58.1)	-2.1 (-16.6)

Source: Authors' estimates.

Note: Column 1 reports impacts for other scenarios relative to the Reference $8 scenario.

the absence of accommodating monetary policy, such large increases in the general price level substantially reduce real purchasing power, causing sizeable decreases in both real consumption and investment. On average, real GNP declines 3.4 percent and 1.6 percent, respectively, in response to the two increases in imported crude oil prices.

There is one case for which a higher crude oil price has little impact on the economy. In the Accelerated Supply and Conservation scenarios, raising the price of imported crude oil from $13 to $16 has virtually no impact on the general price level or real GNP. PIES indicates for the Accelerated Supply and Conservation scenarios that the United States becomes virtually self-sufficient in meeting its domestic energy needs at an imported crude oil price of $13. Only a slight increase in the imported crude oil price above $13 per barrel is required to reduce U.S. oil imports to zero. Once oil imports fall to zero, the domestic crude oil price becomes the marginal price, insulating the economy from the full impact of further increases in foreign crude oil prices.

Higher imported crude oil prices have little impact on the general price level with the Supply Pessimism scenarios, because price controls keep domestic energy prices down, but do affect oil imports and reduce real GNP.

Energy Conservation[g]

Given imported crude oil prices and domestic energy supply conditions, energy conservation has only minor impacts on the economy. Although energy conservation reduces the demand for energy, it has little or no effect on energy prices as long as oil is imported. Consequently, it has little effect on the general price level. The impact on real GNP is also small, although generally favorable. The magnitude of the impact is not surprising considering the small changes in aggregate price levels. For the most part, the small increases in aggregate demand reflect improvement in the balance of trade due to a lower level of oil imports.

The energy conservation impacts reported here may be inaccurate. On the one hand, the DRI model ignores the potentially negative implications of energy conservation on final demand for energy-related goods and services other than gasoline and oil. On the other hand, it ignores the energy-related investment required to conserve energy.

---

[g]The implications of energy conservation can be seen by comparing the Conservation scenarios with the Reference scenarios and the Accelerated Supply and Conservation scenarios with the Accelerated Supply scenarios at given imported crude oil prices.

Domestic Energy Supplies[h]

Given imported crude oil prices and domestic energy demand, the economic impacts of accelerated domestic energy production are usually small. As with energy conservation, energy supply acceleration has little impact on domestic energy prices and the general price level as long as oil is imported. Once again, real GNP increases moderately as reduced oil imports improve the balance of trade.

When increased domestic energy production eliminates the need to import oil, the impact of supply acceleration on real GNP becomes more pronounced. This situation occurs in the Accelerated Supply and Conservation $16 scenario. Relying entirely upon domestically produced oil reduces domestic energy prices and the general price level, inducing a favorable real balance effect. The resulting increases in consumption and investment combine with the improved balance of trade to produce larger increases in real GNP.

Since accelerated energy production has a favorable economic impact, lower than usual energy production would be expected to have an adverse impact on the economy given imported crude oil prices and domestic energy demand. However, price controls on domestically produced crude oil in the Supply Pessimism scenarios sufficiently reduce domestic energy prices and aggregate price levels relative to the Reference scenarios to induce a favorable real balance effect on real GNP that more than offsets the adverse effects of higher oil imports on the balance of trade. Consequently, real GNP is higher in the Supply Pessimism scenarios than in the corresponding Reference scenarios.

Conclusions

The macroeconomic simulations presented in this chapter show that economic conditions can vary considerably from one energy scenario to another. In part, the results reflect the responses of the economy to the energy sector as represented in PIES. However, the results also reflect the methodology used to incorporate the PIES information into the DRI model and the structure of the DRI model.

Because energy prices and oil imports make up the bulk of PIES information incorporated into the DRI model, it is not surprising that economic responses to the various energy scenarios can be attributed to changes in the general price

[h]The implications of different domestic energy supplies can be seen by comparing the Accelerated Supply scenarios with the Reference scenarios, the Accelerated Supply and Conservation scenarios with the Conservation scenarios, and the Supply Pessimism with the Reference scenarios at given imported crude oil prices. Inasmuch as the increases in energy-related investment needed to accelerate domestic energy production were ignored, the impacts reported probably understate the favorable impacts of energy supply acceleration on real GNP.

level and the balance of trade. The DRI model is more sensitive to price changes than it is to changes in imports: the former affect all economic activity through a real balance effect, whereas the latter primarily affect the foreign sector. Consequently, energy scenarios causing the greatest impacts on the general price level tend to have the largest impacts on the economy.

References

1. Federal Energy Administration. *National Energy Outlook* (Washington, D.C.: U.S. Government Printing Office, 1976).

2. Federal Energy Administration. *Project Independence Report* (Washington, D.C.: U.S. Government Printing Office, 1974).

3. Hudson, Edward A. and Dale W. Jorgenson. "U.S. Energy Policy and Economic Growth, 1975-2000." *Bell Journal of Economics and Management Science* 5, no. 2 (Autumn 1974), pp. 461-514.

8

Reconciling Alternative Forecasts of Energy and the Economy
A. Bradley Askin

Introduction

The downturn in U.S. economic activity following the 1973-1974 quadrupling of OPEC oil prices and the Arab oil embargo showed conclusively that energy events have a major, potentially critical, role to play in shaping the performance of the economy.[a] Since 1974, numerous studies have attempted to assess what energy developments are likely with respect to domestic policy, technological change, and the actions of foreign governments, and to forecast what impacts such developments would have on the economy.[b] These studies have differed in three major respects. First, they have identified energy scenarios which differ substantially in technical detail, even though many of the scenarios have seemed superficially similar. Second, the studies have considered different portions of the energy sector and have modeled it in conflicting ways. Third, the studies have recognized and treated interrelationships between the energy sector and other parts of the economy to significantly different degrees.

Explaining discrepancies among the conclusions drawn in the various studies of energy and the economy has been difficult, at least in part, because it has often been impossible to distinguish among the effects produced by the three major differences just described. In this regard, the Malloy analysis of fourteen Federal Energy Administration (FEA) energy scenarios using the long-term Wharton macroeconometric model and the Farman-Lagace analysis of the same scenarios using the Data Resources, Inc. (DRI) macroeconometric model are unique, for they offer an opportunity to focus exclusively on the effects of handling the energy sector in different macroeconomic contexts.[c] This chapter examines the Malloy and Farman-Lagace analyses in detail. One purpose of the

Randall G. Hopkins and William G. Rice performed the new simulations presented in this chapter. A previous version was presented at the Eastern Economic Association Annual Convention, Hartford, Connecticut, April 14-16, 1977.

[a]The embargo lasted from October 1973 to March 1974. For an analysis of the effects that the 1973-1974 oil crisis had on the U.S. economy and a review of other studies on these effects, see Chapter 2 of this volume. For an analogous analysis of the effects that the crisis had on other developed economies, see Chapter 4 of this volume.

[b]For examples of such studies, see [1], [3], [5], and [6].

[c]See Chapters 6 and 7 of this volume.

examination is to determine the extent to which the Malloy and Farman-Lagace results differ. Another is to ascertain, if possible, whether the different treatments given to energy in the long-term Wharton and DRI macroeconometric models or other characteristics of the two models account for whatever differences there are between the Malloy and Farman-Lagace results.

The second section of this chapter briefly reviews the methodologies used by Malloy and by Farman and Lagace, discusses the problems of each methodology, and comments on the limitations common to both methodologies. The third section reviews the Malloy and Farman-Lagace results and reports on extensions of the two analyses undertaken in an attempt to explain the differences between them.

The Methodologies and Their Limitations

Review of the Methodologies

The FEA has developed a comprehensive energy sector simulation model known as PIES (Project Independence Evaluation System) comprised of an econometric demand model, a series of linear constraint supply models, and a fixed point programming model that equilibrates energy demand and supply at minimum cost. PIES simulations provide estimates of energy prices, consumption, domestic production, and imports by eight fuel types, nine regions, and four consuming sectors for any single year.

The Malloy and Farman-Lagace analyses share a common starting point in the form of fourteen separate 1985 PIES simulations prepared by the FEA for its *National Energy Outlook.*[d] Both analyses substitute energy information from these PIES simulations into control solutions of the long-term Wharton and DRI macroeconomic models, respectively, using constant rates of change to interpolate between historical data already in the models and the 1985 PIES information, and resolve the models. The Malloy and Farman-Lagace analyses quickly diverge, however, for they rely on different information from the PIES simulations and use the same information in different ways.

Malloy incorporates a substantial amount of disaggregated PIES detail into a sixty-three-sector input-output matrix imbedded in the long-term Wharton model.[e] Using add factors derived from PIES domestic production information, he modifies the gross product originating variable measuring output in each of

[d]Both PIES and the fourteen energy scenarios considered by Malloy and Farman-Lagace are described at length in [4].

[e]A new version of the long-term Wharton model containing a forty-seven sector input-output matrix is now available. For a description of the version utilized by Malloy, see [7].

four sectors: coal mining; oil and gas extraction; petroleum refining; electric, gas, and sanitary services. The long-term Wharton model contains approximately thirty value-added deflators, most explained as endogenous functions of the sixty-three sector output variables, which are used as sector prices. Malloy lets the model determine the values for nearly all of these sector prices, but uses PIES information to exogenize the two value-added deflators for petroleum refining and for electric, gas, and sanitary services. In addition to adjusting sector outputs and prices in the input-output matrix, Malloy employs PIES import information to exogenize the quantities and prices of imports for three of six import categories that appear in the long-term Wharton model: crude materials, semi-finished manufactures, and finished manufactures. Finally, Malloy utilizes PIES consumption information to exogenize real personal consumption expenditures on gasoline and oil.

The DRI model does not have nearly as much sectoral detail as the long-term Wharton model. Although the DRI model produces forecasts of approximately fifty Federal Reserve Board production indexes, these indexes have little feedback effect on the model and do not constitute a suitable mechanism for introducing energy events into the model. Accordingly, Farman and Lagace rely primarily on prices to transmit energy effects in the DRI model. They use a weighted average of eight prices from PIES to exogenize the WPI for fuel and related products and power. This WPI has direct effects on at least four price deflators in the DRI model and indirect effects on all other ones; in turn, the price deflators influence virtually all final demands. Farman and Lagace also use PIES import information to exogenize four import variables appearing in the DRI model: an average unit value index for crude oil imports: the constant dollar amount of crude oil imports; an average unit value index for refined petroleum product imports; and the constant dollar amount of refined petroleum product imports. As does Malloy, Farman and Lagace exogenize the level of real personal consumption expenditures on gasoline and oil to reflect PIES consumption information.

Limitations of the Methodologies[f]

Difficulties with the Long-term Wharton Model. Two structural features of the long-term Wharton model bias the response of the economy to energy developments in the Malloy analysis. First, the use of CES input substitution functions in the sixty-three-sector input-output matrix implies identical elasticities of substitution between different pairs of inputs used to produce individual goods and services. These elasticities overstate the extent to which goods and services

---

[f]Many of the points made in the following section are discussed in more detail in [1] or Chapters 6 and 7 of this volume.

low in energy content can satisfy final demand. Second, the model contains a simple monetary sector implying an accommodating monetary policy in which the money supply responds in highly elastic fashion and interest rates respond hardly at all to changes in the level of economic activity. Each of these features distorts the magnitude of Malloy's real GNP and inflation impact estimates for various energy events.

Two other characteristics of the long-term Wharton model reduce Malloy's ability to represent energy events. Two of the sector output variables modified by Malloy cover nonenergy industries as well as energy ones, forcing him to make assumptions about these nonenergy components that lead to unavoidable errors when using PIES information to adjust the energy components. Moreover, the gross product originating variables in the model cannot be exogenized. Malloy circumvents this problem by utilizing add factors to modify these variables, but introduces errors into the analysis by doing so, since his procedure yields adjusted sector outputs only initially consistent with PIES domestic energy production information.[g]

Difficulties with the DRI Model. The Farman-Lagace analysis suffers from two serious problems related to the manner in which prices capture the effects of energy events in the DRI model. Although Farman and Lagace calculate a weighted average of eight PIES prices for use as the WPI for fuels and related products and power, only the weighted average appears in the DRI model. Consequently, the individual PIES prices function merely as scalars of one another, and changes in relative prices within the energy sector have no influence on the composition of final demand or the mix of inputs used to produce the goods and services that satisfy final demand.

The DRI model does not differentiate between changes in the WPI for fuel and related products and power that stem from demand shifts and those that stem from supply shifts. It treats both as movements along a demand curve, thereby misrepresenting energy demand shifts as energy supply shifts. Farman and Lagace contend that the failure to separate the two types of energy price change is not significant for goods imported in large quantities, such as oil, since demand and supply shifts for these goods at given world prices affect only the volume of imports and not the level of domestic production. However, this argument assumes that domestic prices change only in response to world price changes and overlooks the fact that U.S. demands for many types of energy are met by domestic production without any need for imports. Inasmuch as the DRI model does not handle the prices of different types of energy

---

[g]Since the gross product originating variables are endogenous in the long-term Wharton model, they change during simulation of the model in response to changes in other variables. Thus, their final values after simulation do not equal their initial values entered into the simulation.

separately, but lumps all of them together in the WPI for fuel and related products and power as already explained, the Farman-Lagace argument does not always hold.

Common Difficulties. In addition to shortcomings specifically related to the long-term Wharton and DRI models, the Malloy and Farman-Lagace analyses share several common limitations. A major difficulty is the partial equilibrium framework in which both analyses are conducted. As the results presented later show, substantially different macroeconomic outcomes are associated with some of the different energy scenarios. Yet the same forecasts of six macroeconomic variables included among the assumptions driving PIES are used for all fourteen of the energy scenarios considered by Malloy and by Farman and Lagace.[h] Iterations of PIES and macroeconomic model simulations to achieve consistency between the macroeconomic forecasts driving PIES and implied by PIES are needed for each scenario. Lacking such iterations, the Malloy and Farman-Lagace analyses can only approximate the economic effects of energy events.

Myriad data deficiencies afflict the Malloy and Farman-Lagace analyses. Major problems arise with prices, since PIES measures them on a constant dollar, city gate basis, whereas the long-term Wharton and DRI models employ price indexes measuring them at various stages of the distribution chain. Transforming the PIES city gate price of interstate natural gas into the wellhead price of intrastate natural gas with historical data in order to compute the WPI for fuel and related products and power for the DRI model is not feasible, for instance, and the PIES price is used on the assumption that the resulting error affects all scenarios the same. Even when prices are defined along more similar lines in PIES and in the variables appearing in the long-term Wharton and DRI models, the absence of historical data on PIES city gate prices complicates their transformation into the appropriate macroeconomic model price indexes.

Owing to the unavailability of PIES information for years other than 1985, Malloy and Farman and Lagace generate data for other years by interpolating between historical data already in the long-term Wharton and DRI models and transformed 1985 PIES information at constant rates of change. Although this approach is reasonable, it leads to arbitrary results. Choosing another adjustment path would obviously alter the Malloy and Farman-Lagace results in the short run prior to 1985 and could easily affect them in the longer run through 1985 and beyond.

That PIES provides no nonenergy information causes problems in both the

---

[h]The six macroeconomic variables used to drive PIES are: real GNP; real disposable income; the unemployment rate; the Federal Reserve Board production index for manufacturing; the Federal Reserve Board production index for chemicals; the Federal Reserve Board production index for primary metals.

long-term Wharton and DRI models. Malloy and Farman and Lagace use the two macroeconomic models precisely in order to identify the nonenergy implications of energy events, of course, but many of these implications cannot be handled without specific nonenergy adjustments to the models. Investment is an excellent case in point. With the long-term Wharton model, where investment is an endogenous function of output at the sector level, PIES information sometimes leads to the wrong changes in nonenergy outputs. For example, there is no way for the model to pick up the building insulation provisions of the FEA conservation scenarios solely on the basis of energy sector information. With the DRI model, where sector outputs have no significant role, and investment responds only to general economic conditions, the problem is even more serious.

Empirical Analysis

The Unadjusted Results

Table 8-1 shows the 1985 real GNP and GNP implicit price deflator levels, together with their 1974-1985 annual rates of change, that Malloy and Farman and Lagace report for each of the fourteen FEA energy scenarios they consider.[i] The real GNP levels are measured in billions of 1958 dollars. The prices appearing at the end of the scenario names refer to the world price of crude oil measured in 1975 constant dollars. Attention should be focused on the differences among scenarios, because the levels and rates of change shown in Table 8-1 depend crucially on the assumptions made in the long-term Wharton and DRI model control solutions underlying the Malloy and Farman-Lagace analyses.

The Malloy and Farman-Lagace results reported in Table 8-1 are similar in two important respects. First, the maximum differences among scenarios are large enough in both analyses to demonstrate that the effects of potential energy events on the economy cannot be ignored. The 1985 levels of real GNP differ among scenarios by as much as $50 billion with both the long-term Wharton and DRI models, implying 1974-1985 annual rates of growth that differ by as much as 0.4 and 0.5 percentage points, respectively. The 1985 price levels differ by as much as 7 percent with the long-term Wharton model and 9 percent with the DRI model, implying 1974-1985 annual rates of inflation that differ by as much as 0.6 and 1.1 percentage points, respectively.

---

[i]The long-term Wharton model results in Table 8-1 reflect a minor modification in the Malloy methodology designed to improve the treatment given to nonenergy components in adjusting certain composite variables on the basis of PIES energy information. The real GNP levels in Table 8-1 are from $6 billion to $11 billion higher than those originally reported by Malloy. The GNP implicit price deflator levels in Table 8-1 are virtually identical to the ones originally reported to Malloy. The original Malloy real GNP and GNP implicit price deflator levels are available in [2].

Table 8-1
Unadjusted 1985 Levels and 1974-1985 Annual Rates of Change

	Malloy Long-Term Wharton Model Simulations				Farman-Lagace DRI Model Simulations			
	Real GNP		GNP Implicit Price Deflator		Real GNP		GNP Implicit Price Deflator	
	1985	1974-1985 Change	1985	1974-1985 Change	1985	1974-1985 Change	1985	1974-1985 Change
Control Solution	$1148	3.1%	3.29	6.2%	$1234	3.8$	2.92	5.0%
Reference $8	1210	3.6	3.31	6.2	1221	3.7	2.91	5.0
Reference $13	1219	3.7	3.40	6.5	1182	3.4	3.08	5.6
Reference $16	1213	3.6	3.44	6.6	1160	3.2	3.18	5.9
Conservation $8	1211	3.6	3.23	6.0	1227	3.7	2.89	4.9
Conservation $13	1216	3.6	3.33	6.3	1184	3.4	3.09	5.6
Conservation $16	1218	3.7	3.40	6.5	1164	3.2	3.23	6.0
Accelerated Supply $8	1228	3.7	3.33	6.3	1229	3.7	2.92	5.0
Accelerated Supply $13	1241	3.8	3.40	6.5	1191	3.4	3.14	5.7
Accelerated Supply $16	1240	3.8	3.42	6.6	–	–	–	–
Accelerated Supply/Conservation $8	1222	3.7	3.24	6.0	1232	3.8	2.91	5.0
Accelerated Supply/Conservation $13	1226	3.7	3.32	6.3	1186	3.4	3.14	5.7
Accelerated Supply/Conservation $16	1235	3.8	3.33	6.3	1191	3.4	3.16	5.8
Supply Pessimism $13	1195	3.5	3.31	6.2	1183	3.4	2.96	5.2
Supply Pessimism $16	1189	3.4	3.34	6.3	1169	3.3	2.98	5.2

Source: Author's estimates and A. Bradley Askin et al., "An Empirical Analysis of the Relationship between Energy and the Economy," *Journal of Energy and Development*, 6, no. 2 (Spring, 1977), pp. 252-6.

Notes: Real GNP is measured in billions of 1958 dollars. The base year for the GNP implicit price deflator is 1958 (1958 = 1.0). The 1974–1985 rates of change are geometric mean annual rates of change. The DRI model solution algorithm did not converge for the Accelerated Supply $16 scenario.

Second, the differences between many scenarios and the Reference $13 scenario, the case that comes closest to representing a business as usual continuation of the status quo, are quite small. Such minor differences indicate that changes in domestic energy policy designed to improve the current energy situation need not have significantly adverse effects on the economy. Ascertaining the statistical significance of the differences among scenarios implicit in Table 8-1 is impossible, of course, inasmuch as the long-term Wharton and DRI models provide point estimates without corresponding error measures. However, economic theory suggests that the partial equilibrium framework of the Malloy and Farman-Lagace analyses exaggerates the true differences among scenarios by ignoring feedback effects from the economy to the demand for energy. Differences in the level of economic activity imply differences in the demand for energy, which in turn cause price responses and real balance effects partially offsetting the original differences in the level of economic activity.

Given that energy conservation proposals have been vociferously opposed on the grounds that they would mean zero growth, recession, or worse, the scenarios involving conservation represent an especially noteworthy set of cases where the Malloy and Farman-Lagace analyses indicate small differences among scenarios. Out of eleven implicit comparisons in Table 8-1 involving Conservation versus Reference scenarios or Accelerated Supply and Conservation versus Accelerated Supply scenarios for common world prices of crude oil, 1985 real GNP is higher in the scenario including conservation six times and lower in that scenario by as much as $10 billion only once. Such evidence does not support the charge that energy conservation has adverse effects on the economy.[j]

The Malloy and Farman-Lagace results shown in Table 8-1 diverge in two ways. Energy supply assumptions have larger impacts in the long-term Wharton model than in the DRI model, as can be seen by comparing the scenarios including energy supply assumptions with the appropriate ones that do not.[k] The add factor adjustments Malloy makes to sector outputs produce a positive correlation between domestic energy production and real GNP with the long-term Wharton model. This relationship has considerable intuitive appeal, although it cannot be determined from the long-term Wharton model whether the magnitudes reported in Table 8-1 realistically reflect production possibilities. The Farman-Lagace reliance on prices leads to energy supply impacts that mainly reflect import

---

[j]The absence of nonenergy information poses two problems in evaluating the energy conservation scenarios. First, the upward pressure that conservation programs would place on the prices of certain goods and services, such as insulation materials, is ignored. Second, the expansion of production and employment in certain sectors, such as construction, is also ignored. Fortunately, these two forces imply opposite effects on real GNP, so that ignoring them leads to partially offsetting errors.

[k]The relevant comparisons are those involving the Accelerated Supply versus Reference scenarios, the Accelerated Supply and Conservation versus Conservation scenarios, and the Supply Pessimism versus Reference scenarios for common world prices of crude oil.

differences and are small enough to ignore, because the DRI model does not take into account the effects that energy prices have on domestic energy production.

Changes in the world price of crude oil have quite different impacts in the Malloy and Farman-Lagace analyses. Higher world crude oil prices accelerate inflation in both analyses, but have opposite effects on 1985 real GNP. With the long-term Wharton model, in which implicit accommodating monetary policy minimizes the adverse real balance effects that higher prices have on aggregate demand, higher world crude oil prices stimulate domestic energy production and reduce energy imports enough to slightly raise 1985 real GNP with most energy policies. With the DRI model, in which domestic energy production is ignored, higher world crude oil prices produce adverse real balance effects that outweigh energy import declines and significantly reduce 1985 real GNP with all energy policies. Changes in the world price of crude oil consistently lead to 1985 real GNP impacts of considerably smaller magnitude with the long-term Wharton model than with the DRI model. As a result, changes in the world price of crude oil appear to be less important relative to changes in energy policy with the long-term Wharton model than with the DRI model.

The Adjusted Results

Table 8-2 shows the 1985 real GNP and GNP implicit price deflator levels, together with their 1974-1985 annual rates of change, estimated with modified versions of the Malloy and Farman-Lagace methodologies. The adjusted Malloy results reflect a second iteration of the long-term Wharton model simulations based on modified add factors for the sector output variables. These modified add factors yield final values of the sector output variables that are consistent with PIES production information. As pointed out earlier, only the initial values of the sector output variables are consistent with PIES production information in the single iteration Malloy analysis. The adjusted Farman-Lagace results reflect successive iterations of the DRI model simulations that use add factor adjustments in free reserves to force the federal funds rate within 0.1 percentage points of its level in the DRI model control solution for every year between 1974 and 1985. The imposed stickiness in interest rates produces an accommodating monetary policy similar to that implicit in the long-term Wharton model.

On average, the 1985 real GNP levels reported for the long-term Wharton model in Table 8-2 are lower than those reported in Table 8-1 by $76 billion, with reductions for individual scenarios ranging between $48 billion and $99 billion. In contrast, the 1985 real GNP levels presented for the DRI model in Table 8-2 are higher than those presented in Table 8-1 by an average of only $7 billion, with the impacts on individual scenarios ranging from -$7 billion to $21 billion. With both models the impact on individual scenarios varies

Table 8-2
Adjusted 1985 Levels and 1974–1985 Annual Rates of Change

Scenario	Malloy Long-Term Wharton Model Simulations				Farman-Lagace DRI Model Simulations			
	Real GNP		GNP Implicit Price Deflator		Real GNP		GNP Implicit Price Deflator	
	1985	1974–1985 Change	1985	1974–1985 Change	1985	1974–1985 Change	1985	1974–1985 Change
Control Solution	$1148	3.1%	3.29	6.2%	$1234	3.8%	2.92	5.0%
Reference $8	1111	2.8	3.36	6.4	1215	3.6	2.91	5.0
Reference $13	1163	3.2	3.27	6.1	1195	3.5	3.09	5.6
Reference $16	1165	3.2	3.43	6.4	1181	3.4	3.21	5.9
Conservation $8	1113	2.8	3.27	6.1	1221	3.7	2.89	4.9
Conservation $13	1142	3.0	3.31	6.2	1196	3.5	3.11	5.6
Conservation $16	1162	3.2	3.38	6.4	1185	3.4	3.24	6.0
Accelerated Supply $8	1150	3.1	3.29	6.2	1229	3.7	2.93	5.1
Accelerated Supply $13	1178	3.3	3.34	6.3	1209	3.6	3.16	5.8
Accelerated Supply $16	1177	3.3	3.36	6.4	—	—	—	—
Accelerated Supply/Conservation $8	1125	2.9	3.22	6.0	1232	3.8	2.92	5.0
Accelerated Supply/Conservation $13	1143	3.1	3.28	6.2	1206	3.6	3.14	5.7
Accelerated Supply/Conservation $16	1154	3.1	3.27	6.1	1208	3.6	3.16	5.8
Supply Pessimism $13	1108	2.8	3.32	6.3	1177	3.3	2.96	5.2
Supply Pessimism $16	1111	2.8	3.36	6.4	1162	3.2	2.98	5.2

Source: Author's estimates.

Notes: Real GNP is measured in billions of 1958 dollars. The base year for the GNP implicit price deflator is 1958 (1958 = 1.0). The 1974–1985 rates of change are geometric mean annual rates of change. The DRI model solution algorithm did not converge for the Accelerated Supply $16 scenario.

inversely with the world price of crude oil, but follows no clear pattern with respect to domestic energy policy. The 1985 GNP implicit price deflator levels shown in Table 8-2 are close to those shown in Table 8-1 for nearly all cases and therefore require no discussion.

Despite the significantly different 1985 real GNP levels reported for the long-term Wharton model in Tables 8-2 and 8-1, the adjusted Malloy and Farman-Lagace results are similar and dissimilar in basically the same ways as are the unadjusted Malloy and Farman-Lagace results. The maximum 1985 real GNP differences among scenarios are more than $70 billion with both adjusted analyses, but differences between many scenarios and the Reference $13 case continue to be quite small with both analyses. Energy conservation has somewhat less favorable effects than before: it leads to slightly higher 1985 real GNP in five of eleven relevant comparisons, but causes declines of more than $20 billion in four comparisons. Energy supply assumptions continue to have plausible direct impacts on 1985 real GNP with the long-term Wharton model and small impacts that can be ignored with the DRI model. Increases in the world price of crude oil now raise 1985 real GNP for all domestic energy policies, instead of just for most of them, with the long-term Wharton model and continue to lower it for all energy policies with the DRI model.

Summary and Conclusions

The Malloy and Farman-Lagace analyses employ long-term Wharton and DRI model simulations, respectively, to assess the macroeconomic implications of fourteen FEA energy scenarios in a partial equilibrium framework. Because they use different macroeconometric models, the two analyses represent the interrelationships between the energy sector and other portions of the economy in different fashion. Consequently, each analysis suffers from certain unique problems in addition to the ones shared in common.

Despite their limitations, the Malloy and Farman-Lagace analyses provide useful insights into the macroeconomic impacts associated with alternative energy scenarios. Both analyses show that energy events have impacts on the economy which are too large to ignore. Yet, both analyses also show that changes in energy policy designed to improve the current energy situation need not have significantly adverse impacts on the economy. For example, both analyses indicate that energy conservation would not create economic chaos. The two analyses produce contradictory results with respect to the impacts that energy supply and world crude oil price changes have.

It is not possible to disentangle the influences that the structures of the long-term Wharton and DRI models versus the representation of energy events in the two models have on the Malloy and Farman-Lagace analyses. On the one hand, the magnitude of the 1985 real GNP reductions reported for the long-term

Wharton model in Table 8-2 relative to Table 8-1 demonstrates the importance of the representation given to the interrelationships between the energy sector and the economy. In this context, the much smaller differences between the 1985 real GNP levels reported for the DRI model in Tables 8-2 and 8-1 may simply indicate that monetary policy has more to do with macroeconomic model specification in general than with treating the interrelationships between the energy sector and the economy. On the other hand, the consistency of the similarities and dissimilarities between the adjusted Malloy and Farman-Lagace results reported in Table 8-2 with the similarities and dissimilarities between the unadjusted Malloy and Farman-Lagace results reported in Table 8-1 suggests that the structures of the long-term Wharton and DRI models are at least as important as the exact representation of energy events in the two models.

References

1. Askin, A. Bradley. "The Macroeconometric Implications of Alternative Energy Scenarios." In Askin and Kraft, eds., *Econometric Dimensions of Energy Demand and Supply* (Lexington, Mass.: D.C. Health and Company, 1976), pp. 91-109.

2. Askin, A. Bradley et al. "An empirical Analysis of the Relationship Between Energy and the Economy." *Journal of Energy and Development*, 2, no. 2 (Spring 1977), pp. 252-6.

3. Behling, David J., Jr., Robert Dullion, and Edward Hudson. *The Relationship of Energy Growth to Economic Growth under Alternative Energy Policies*, BNL50500 (Upton, New York: Brookhaven National Laboratory, 1976).

4. Federal Energy Administration. *National Energy Outlook* (Washington, D.C.: U.S. Government Printing Office, 1976).

5. Freeman, S. David et al. *A Time to Choose America's Energy Future*. Final Report of the Energy Policy Project of the Ford Foundation (Cambridge, Mass.: Ballinger Publishing Company, 1974).

6. Hudson, Edward A. and Dale W. Jorgenson. "U.S. Energy Policy and Economic Growth, 1975-2000." *Bell Journal of Economics and Management Science*, 5, no. 2 (Autumn 1974), pp. 461-514.

7. Wharton Econometric Forecasting Associates, Inc. "Annual and Industrial Model Equations." Philadelphia, Pennsylvania, June 1975.

Alternative Energy Futures and the Structure of Employment in the U.S. Economy
Ronald F. Earley and Malek M. Mohtadi

Introduction

Changes in the world price of oil and shifts in domestic energy policy act on various economic units in different ways by affecting the level and composition of final demand so as to alter industrial output and employment requirements within the economy. This chapter examines the impacts that changes in the world price of crude oil and shifts in domestic energy policy would have on 1985 sector and occupation employment levels.

The employment impact analysis is performed with an input-output (I-O) model projected to represent the economy in 1985. Alternative vectors of final demand, derived from macroeconomic simulations of the U.S. economy, are used to drive the I-O model for each of thirteen alternative Project Independence Evaluation System (PIES) energy scenarios developed by the Federal Energy Administration (FEA). Simulations of the I-O model are performed to forecast 1985 employment levels for 129 sectors and 470 occupations. The disaggregated sector and occupation employment levels are then aggregated into employment totals for ten major sectors and nine major occupations for evaluation purposes.

The chapter consists of two major sections. The first section describes the methodology used to determine the employment impacts and discusses its limitations. The second section evaluates the sector and occupation employment impacts of changes in the world price of crude oil and shifts in domestic energy policy. Both actual and percentage employment differences among scenarios are considered. A final section summarizes the major findings.

Methodology

The analysis is based on the BLS I-O model, which projects 1985 employment on a jobs basis for 129 sectors of the economy by 470 occupations.[a] At the core of the model are two matrices. A direct coefficients matrix gives the direct dollar

---

[a]The BLS I-O model was originally developed for analyzing labor-related issues. Based on 1963 benchmark interindustry data collected by the Bureau of Economic Analysis in the U.S. Department of Commerce, it is currently being updated with 1967 benchmark interindustry data published in 1974. For a full description of the model, see [3, pp. 70–79 and 139–49].

inputs from other sectors required per dollar of output for each sector. An inverse matrix shows the total dollar outputs of other sectors required directly and indirectly per dollar of final demand satisfied by each sector. Other elements of the model include a bridge table for distributing final demand to the 129 sectors, projected employment-output ratios for the 129 sectors, and an occupation matrix reflecting the employment mix among 470 occupations for each of the 129 sectors.

Simulation Procedure

Nineteen components of final demand for each energy scenario were extracted from simulations of the Data Resources, Inc. (DRI) model.[b] These nineteen components of final demand were converted into 1963 dollars with implicit price deflators and distributed among the 129 sectors of the I-O model with a bridge table. The bridge table generated a bill of goods to drive the I-O model by distributing each component of final demand to the appropriate producing sectors, including a reallocation of transportation costs and wholesale and retail mark-ups from producing sectors to the appropriate transportation and trade sectors, on the basis of historical relationships. The bill of goods was multiplied by an employment matrix to determine the sector employment levels required to satisfy final demand. The employment matrix was formed by multiplying each row of the inverse matrix by the employment-output ratio for the sector represented by that row.

To make the sector employment levels sensitive to changes in productivity across scenarios, productivity forecasts from the DRI model simulations were used to override the fixed productivity rate inherent in the BLS employment-output ratios. Adjustments were made for each sector with the equation

$$E_j^* = E_j \ \frac{PI - \Delta PI}{PI} \quad , j = 1, \ldots , 129 \qquad (9.1)$$

where E_j^* is adjusted sector employment for the jth sector, E_j is unadjusted sector employment for the jth sector, PI is the aggregate BLS productivity index, and ΔPI is the algebraic difference between the DRI macroeconomic model simulation productivity index and the BLS aggregate productivity index.[c]

---

[b]Analyses similar to that reported on in this chapter have been performed based on simulations of the Wharton long-term macroeconomic model and could be performed based on any vector of final demands. For a description of the DRI macroeconomic model simulation procedures, see Chapter 6 in this book.

[c]The employment-output ratios in the BLS I-O model are based on the projection that productivity in the private economy, as measured by private real GNP in 1958 dollars per man-hour, will increase between 1972 and 1985 at an annual rate of 2.51 percent. The DRI model employs a productivity index which has the value 1.115 in 1975. Applying the BLS projection of productivity growth to the 1975 value of the productivity index in the DRI model gives a 1985 BLS productivity index value of 1.429. Thus, PI = 1.429 in Equation (9.1).

For evaluation purposes, the 129 adjusted sector employment levels were aggregated into employment totals for ten major sectors: Agriculture, Forestry, and Fisheries; Mining; Construction; Manufacturing; Transportation; Communications and Public Utilities; Wholesale and Retail Trade; Finance, Insurance, and Real Estate; Services; and Government Enterprises. The Government Enterprises sector includes government agencies deriving 50 percent or more of their revenues from sales to the public (for example, the U.S. Post Office). The I-O model does not treat government employment in general, so the summation of employment in the ten major sectors gives employment for the private economy.

The adjusted sector employment levels were transformed into 470 occupation employment levels with the occupation matrix. Multiplying the occupation matrix by the adjusted sector employment levels gave the occupation employment levels required to satisfy final demand. For evaluation purposes, the 470 occupation employment levels were aggregated into employment totals for nine major occupations: Professional, Technical, and Kindred Workers; Managers, Officials, and Proprietors; Sales Workers; Clerical Workers; Crafts and Kindred Workers; Operatives; Service Workers; Nonfarm Laborers; and Farmers and Farm Workers.[d]

Limitations

Essentially a final demand determination model without a detailed supply sector, the DRI model lacks a mechanism for constraining domestic energy supplies to be consistent with PIES information. This limitation reduced the quality of the macroeconomic results used to drive the I-O model and led to employment levels for energy-producing sectors not always consistent with those required to produce the domestic energy outputs forecasted by PIES.[e]

Transformation of the nineteen DRI macroeconomic model final demand components into the 129 sector bill of goods which drives the I-O model was undertaken with the same bridge table for all scenarios. As a result, the distribution of the nineteen individual final demand components was the same in all scenarios. This approach did not take into account the way the changes in relative energy prices examined would affect the mixes of individual goods and services that constitute each of the nineteen final demand components and yield different bills of goods than does the single bridge table utilized. The availability of more disaggregated final demand data from the DRI model would reduce the problems associated with using the same bridge table for all scenarios, of course.

Technical coefficients for 1980 and 1985 projected by BLS in 1973 did not

---

[d]Since the occupation employment levels are derived from, and consistent with, the sector employment levels, summing the nine major occupations gives employment for the private economy.

[e]For discussions of the limitations of the DRI model results, see Chapters 6 and 8 in this book.

reflect the 1973-1974 Arab oil embargo. Recognition of this fact and the 1974-1975 recession prompted BLS to project new technical coefficients for 1980 and 1985 that reflect the demise of cheap and plentiful energy supplies.[f] However, improvements are still needed in these revised technical coefficients, including means of adjusting them across scenarios to allow for substitution among inputs.[g]

Closely related to the problem of fixed technical coefficients is the implicit assumption of fixed productivity in all scenarios. Although the incorporation of DRI model productivity changes across scenarios overcame this assumption, in some cases the DRI model forecasted quite large productivity changes that must be viewed with skepticism. A possible solution would be to constrain the productivity equation in the DRI macroeconomic model to give more reasonable results, but this approach must await additional work to develop the appropriate constraints.

The employment levels generated by the I-O model reflected sector output levels needed to satisfy particular final demand levels. The analysis presupposed the existence of a labor force possessing the needed mix of skills. The effects that changes in wage rates and other factors across scenarios would have on the supply of labor were not explicitly addressed. The proper mix of skills implied by certain energy scenarios may not be available, particularly for those scenarios in which large increases in the number of highly skilled workers are needed.

Employment Impacts

The Energy Scenarios

The thirteen PIES energy scenarios selected for analysis were developed by the FEA in conjunction with *National Energy Outlook* and are described in detail in that document.[h] The scenarios combine assumptions about the price of imported crude oil with assumptions about domestic energy policy. The scenarios utilize three world prices of crude oil: $8, $13 and $16 per barrel in 1975 dollars. Five domestic energy policy situations are considered: Reference, or business as usual, conditions; Conservation conditions involving nonprice energy demand restraints; Accelerated Supply conditions, designed to encourage domestic energy production; Accelerated Supply and Conservation conditions,

---

[f]The revised BLS projections are described in [2].

[g]For indirect evidence on the potential importance of future substitution among inputs in relation to energy events, see Chapter 3 in this book.

[h]See Appendix E in [1].

combining the energy demand and supply assumptions of the previous two situations; and Supply Pessimism conditions, assuming unfavorable geologic finding rates, a domestic crude oil price ceiling of $9 per barrel in 1975 dollars, and the imposition of severe environmental constraints on domestic energy production.

Changes in the World Price of Crude Oil

Table 9-1 shows for the Reference scenarios the impacts that changes in the price of imported crude oil have on employment, using the convention that the price of imported crude oil changes from $13 to either $8 or $16.[i]

Relative to the Reference $13 scenario, employment in the private economy is higher by 162,000 jobs, a 0.2 percent difference, and lower by 140,000 jobs, a -0.2 percent difference, with the Reference $8 and $16 scenarios, respectively. These employment differences are slightly smaller on average than the real GNP differences of 3.2 percent and -1.9 percent, respectively, that cause them, reflecting an amelioration of the employment effects implied by the real GNP effects through productivity adjustments. The elasticity measure suggests that both employment and real GNP respond proportionally less when the price of imported oil falls to $8 than when it rises to $16.

As Table 9-1 shows, the distribution of employment among major sectors and occupations in the private economy shifts significantly when the price of imported crude oil changes from $13 to either $8 or $16. Four of ten major sectors and four of nine major occupations experience employment changes in the opposite direction than does the total private economy for both increases and decreases in the world price of crude oil. A few sectors and occupations experience large employment impacts, but most experience relatively minor impacts. As can be seen from the elasticity measure, employment in most sectors and occupations responds proportionally less when the price of imported crude oil falls to $8 than when it rises to $16, with Mining the only notable exception to this general pattern.

Employment gains and losses for the ten major sectors total 544,000 and 382,000 jobs, respectively, for the Reference $8 scenario relative to the Reference $13 scenario. Manufacturing and Construction gain the most jobs. Services loses the most jobs by a wide margin. Construction, Manufacturing, and Transportation gain the most employment in percent terms, while Mining suffers by far the largest employment loss in percent terms. According to PIES, domestic

---

[i]The Reference $13 scenario comes closer than any other to representing a status quo continuation of the current energy situation. In Table 9-1 the direction of change does not affect the elasticities reported, but does affect the sign of the actual changes and the sign and magnitude of the percent changes reported.

Table 9-1
Net Employment Impacts of Changes in the World Price of Crude Oil

Sector Impacts

	Real GNP 1958 $ (Billions)	Productivity Index	Adjusted Private Employment	Agricultural Forestry, and Fisheries	Mining	Construction	Manufacturing	Transportation	Communication and Public Utilities	Wholesale and Retail Trade	Finance, Insurance, and Real Estate	Services	Government Enterprises
Actual Change													
Reference $8	38.7	0.042	162	10	-61	166	321	28	–	19	-69	-246	-6
Reference $16	-21.9	-0.022	-140	-3	22	-88	-168	-19	-3	6	32	82	-1
Percent Change													
Reference $8	3.2	3.0	0.2	0.5	-10.8	3.4	1.6	1.1	–	0.1	-1.3	-1.2	-0.4
Reference $16	-1.9	-1.6	-0.2	-0.1	4.0	-1.8	-0.9	-0.8	-0.1	–	0.6	0.4	–
Elasticity													
Reference $8	-0.0676	-0.0613	-0.0042	-0.0092	0.2389	-0.0701	-0.0336	-0.0235	–	0.0016	0.0268	0.0168	-0.0079
Reference $16	-0.0899	-0.0754	-0.0077	-0.0058	0.1836	-0.0879	-0.0406	-0.0367	-0.0067	0.0009	0.0280	0.0183	-0.0029

Occupation Impacts

	Professional, Technical, and Kindred Workers	Managers, Officials, and Proprietors	Sales Workers	Clerical Workers	Crafts and Kindred Workers	Operatives	Service Workers	Nonfarm Laborers	Farmers and Farm Workers
Actual Change									
Reference $8	-40	6	-4	-34	134	123	-61	30	8
Reference $16	5	-7	4	4	-77	-71	21	-17	-2
Percent Change									
Reference $8	-0.4	0.1	-0.1	-0.2	1.2	0.9	-0.6	0.8	0.4
Reference $16	0.1	-0.1	0.1	–	-0.7	-0.5	0.2	-0.5	-0.1
Elasticity									
Reference $8	0.0079	-0.0012	0.0012	0.0042	-0.0247	-0.0193	0.0032	-0.0168	-0.0096
Reference $16	0.0019	-0.0029	0.0029	0.0009	-0.0328	-0.0261	0.0106	-0.0222	-0.0048

Source: Authors' estimates.

Note: Impacts are shown in thousands of jobs relative to the Reference $13 scenario.

production of coal, natural gas, and crude oil is lower with the Reference $8 scenario than with the Reference $13 scenario by 14.0 percent, 8.4 percent, and 18.0 percent, respectively. The average of these production declines is broadly consistent with the 10.8 percent decline in Mining employment even though the latter is offset somewhat by a rise in real GNP.[j]

Employment gains and losses for the ten major sectors total 142,000 and 282,000 jobs, respectively, for the Reference $16 scenario relative to the Reference $13 scenario. Services; Mining; and Finance, Insurance and Real Estate gain almost all the jobs. Manufacturing and Construction lose 168,000 and 88,000 jobs, respectively. Mining gains by far the most employment in percent terms, while Construction, Manufacturing, and Transportation lose the most in percent terms. Domestic production of coal, natural gas, and crude oil is higher with the Reference $16 scenario than with the Reference $13 scenario by 4.4 percent, 1.1 percent, and 7.9 percent, respectively. The average of these production changes is consistent with the 4.0 percent higher Mining employment level in the Reference $16 scenario relative to the Reference $13 scenario.

Employment gains and losses for the nine major occupations total 301,000 and 139,000 jobs, respectively, for the Reference $8 scenario relative to the Reference $13 scenario. Crafts and Kindred Workers and Operatives gain the most jobs, while Service Workers lose the most jobs. These same three occupations and Nonfarm Laborers experience the largest employment changes in percent terms. Employment gains and losses for the nine major occupations total 34,000 and 174,000 jobs, respectively, for the Reference $16 scenario relative to the Reference $13 scenario. Crafts and Kindred Workers, Operatives, Service Workers, and Nonfarm Laborers experience the largest employment changes in both absolute and percent terms.

Changes in Domestic Energy Policy

Table 9-2 shows for a $13 price of imported crude oil the impacts that changes in domestic energy policy have on employment, using the convention that the Reference $13 scenario gives way to other conditions.

Relative to the Reference $13 scenario, employment in the private economy is lower by 69,000 jobs, a -0.1 percent difference, with the Conservation $13 scenario; higher by 977,000 jobs, a 1.2 percent difference, with the Accelerated Supply $13 scenario; higher by 576,000 jobs, a 0.7 percent difference, with the Accelerated Supply and Conservation $13 scenario; and lower by 1,009,000 jobs, a -1.2 percent difference, with the Supply Pessimism $13 scenario. With

---

[j]As discussed in the limitations part of the methodology section, the I-O model generates sector employment levels on the basis of final demand. There is no mechanism to constrain Mining employment to be consistent with PIES information.

Table 9–2
Net Employment Impacts of Changes in Domestic Energy Policy

Sector Impacts

	Real GNP 1958 $ (Billions)	Productivity Index	Adjusted Private Employment	Agricultural, Forestry, and Fisheries	Mining	Construction	Manufacturing	Transportation	Communication and Public Utilities	Wholesale and Retail Trade	Finance, Insurance, and Real Estate	Services	Government Enterprises
Actual Change													
Conservation $13	1.8	0.002	-69	-4	24	-10	4	-8	–	-72	4	-7	–
Acc. Supply $13	9.0	-0.008	977	27	77	-46	225	25	25	378	72	176	18
Acc. S/Con. $13	4.4	-0.006	576	8	67	-42	141	6	18	208	51	107	12
Supply Pess. $13	1.3	0.022	-1009	-23	-97	107	-116	-19	-27	-385	-99	-326	-24
Percent Change													
Conservation $13	0.2	0.1	-0.1	-0.2	4.2	-0.2		-0.3		-0.3	0.1		
Acc. Supply $13	0.8	-0.6	1.2	1.2	13.7	-0.9	1.1	1.0	1.3	1.7	1.3	0.8	1.2
Acc. S/Con. $13	0.4	-0.4	0.7	0.4	11.9	-0.9	0.7	0.2	0.9	1.0	0.9	0.5	0.8
Supply Pess. $13	0.1	1.6	-1.2	-1.0	-17.1	2.2	-0.6	-0.8	-1.4	-1.8	-1.8	-1.6	-1.6

Occupation Impacts

	Professional, Technical, and Kindred Workers	Managers Officials and Proprietors	Sales Workers	Clerical Workers	Crafts and Kindred Workers	Operatives	Service Workers	Nonfarm Laborers	Farmers and Farm Workers
Actual Change									
Conservation $13	-1	-12	-15	-12	-7	-2	-12	-5	-3
Acc. Supply $13	112	118	104	197	95	178	112	40	21
Acc. S/Con. $13	70	70	60	121	53	110	65	21	6
Supply Pess. $13	-146	-126	-110	-231	-52	-142	-153	-31	-18
Percent Change									
Conservation $13	–	-0.1	-0.2	-0.1	-0.1	–	-0.1	-0.1	-0.2
Acc. Supply $13	1.1	1.3	1.6	1.3	0.8	1.4	1.2	1.1	1.2
Acc. S/Con. $13	0.7	0.8	0.9	0.8	0.5	0.8	0.7	0.6	0.4
Supply Pess. $13	-1.4	-1.4	-1.7	-1.5	-0.5	-1.1	-1.6	-0.8	-1.0

Source: Authors' estimates.
Note: Impacts are shown in thousands of jobs relative to the Reference $13 scenario.

one exception, these employment impacts are larger in magnitude than those associated with changes in the world price of crude oil even though the real GNP impacts of changes in domestic energy policy are smaller than those of changes in the world price of crude oil. This result can be attributed to differences in the way productivity responds to changes in domestic energy policy versus changes in the world price of crude oil. Productivity moves proportionally to real GNP and largely negates potential employment effects when the world price of crude oil changes, but tends to magnify the employment effects when domestic energy policy changes.[k]

Employment shifts differently among the major sectors and occupations when domestic energy policy changes than when the world price of crude oil changes. Except for the Conservation $13 scenario, sector and occupation employment levels tend to change in the same direction when domestic energy policy changes. In contrast, they tend to change in offsetting fashion when the price of imported crude oil changes. Two or three sectors absorb a large portion of the net impact on employment in the private economy when domestic energy policy changes, as when the price of imported crude oil changes, but the impacts on occupations are fairly evenly distributed.

The private economy, sector, and occupation employment impacts for the Accelerated Supply and Conservation $13 scenario relative to the Reference $13 scenario are all smaller than the sum of these impacts for the Conservation $13 scenario and Accelerated Supply $13 scenario considered separately relative to the Reference $13 scenario. This result reflects the fact that the conservation and accelerated supply policies interact when combined so as to affect the level and composition of final demand differently than would be expected on the basis of their separate effects.

Employment gains and losses for the ten major sectors total 32,000 and 101,000 jobs, respectively, for the Conservation $13 scenario relative to the Reference $13 scenario. Mining gains the most jobs, while Wholesale and Retail Trade loses the most. Mining experiences the largest employment impact in percent terms, with all other sectors experiencing small impacts. Domestic production of coal and natural gas is lower by 3.2 percent and 2.2 percent, respectively, while domestic production of crude oil is higher by 0.9 percent. The average of these production changes is inconsistent with the 4.2 percent increase in Mining employment. The discrepancy is not easily explained by the impact on real GNP either, because the small increase in real GNP reflects

---

[k]The DRI model treats productivity as a function of real GNP in the private economy and the gross effective capital stock of private nonresidential structures and producers durable equipment. Given this function, changes in the world price of crude oil cause larger productivity changes than do changes in domestic energy policy. First, changes in the world price of crude oil have larger impacts on real GNP. Second, changes in the world price of crude oil mainly affect investment, and thus the gross effective capital stock, while changes in domestic energy policy mainly affect imports and net exports.

a reduction in imports rather than any increase in domestic expenditures and production. Employment is lower in all nine major occupations, with the loss in jobs generally small.

Employment gains and losses for the ten major sectors and nine major occupations for the Accelerated Supply $13 scenario and Accelerated Supply and Conservation $13 scenario relative to the Reference $13 scenario are quite similar. In both cases employment is lower in Construction and higher in all other sectors. Wholesale and Retail Trade, Manufacturing, and Services gain the most jobs in both cases, with Mining gaining by far the most employment in percent terms. Relative to the Reference $13 scenario, domestic production of coal is lower by 2.1 percent and 2.5 percent with the Accelerated Supply $13 scenario and Accelerated Supply and Conservation $13 scenario, respectively. Domestic natural gas production is higher by 13.6 percent and 9.5 percent, respectively, and domestic crude oil production is higher by 26.8 percent and 15.5 percent, respectively. The averages of these two sets of production changes are broadly consistent with the Mining employment gains of 13.7 percent and 11.9 percent with the two scenarios. Employment is higher for all nine major occupations in both cases, with Clerical Workers and Operatives gaining the most jobs.

Except for Construction, which gains 107,000 jobs, employment is lower in all major sectors with the Supply Pessimism $13 scenario than with the Reference $13 scenario. Wholesale and Retail Trade loses 385,000 jobs, and Services loses another 326,000 jobs, while Mining suffers by far the largest employment loss in percent terms. Domestic production of coal, natural gas, and crude oil is lower by 12.5 percent, 19.5 percent, and 30.8 percent, respectively. The average of these production changes is broadly consistent with the Mining employment reduction of 17.1 percent, which is kept from being worse by a marginal rise in real GNP. Employment losses are spread fairly evenly across all nine major occupations.

Simultaneous Changes in the World Price of Crude Oil and
Domestic Energy Policy

Table 9-3 shows for six scenarios the impact that simultaneous changes in the world price of crude oil and domestic energy policy have on employment, using the convention that all changes occur from the Reference $13 scenario. All of the impacts reported in Table 9-3 diverge substantially from the sums of the relevant impacts reported in Table 9-1 and 9-2 for changes in the world price of crude oil and domestic energy policy considered separately. This outcome reflects an interaction of the two types of change that affect the level and composition of final demand and productivity differently from what would be expected on the basis of the two types of change considered separately.

Table 9-3
Net Employment Impacts of Simultaneous Changes in the World Price of Crude Oil and Domestic Energy Policy

Sector Impacts

	Real GNP 1958 $ (Billions)	Productivity Index	Adjusted Private Employment	Agriculture, Forestry and Fisheries	Mining	Construction	Manufacturing	Transportation	Communication and Public Utilities	Wholesale and Retail Trade	Finance Insurance, and Real Estate	Services	Government Enterprises
Actual Change													
Conservation $8	44.8	0.050	-37	11	-43	168	340	17	-2	-136	-79	-304	-9
Acc. Supply $8	47.0	0.039	758	27	-13	144	461	47	17	221	-27	-126	7
Acc. S/Con. $8	49.8	0.046	413	24	3	138	438	30	10	13	-43	-201	1
Conservation $16	-18.5	-0.030	440	-1	60	-135	-35	-10	17	208	80	241	15
Acc. S/Con. $16	8.7	-0.012	1175	24	85	-64	293	24	33	421	90	245	24
Supply Pess. $16	-13.0	0.015	-1471	-37	-115	89	-291	-38	-38	-541	-113	-355	-32
Percent Change													
Conservation $8	3.8	3.5	—	0.5	-7.6	3.5	1.7	0.7	-0.1	-0.6	-1.5	-1.5	-0.6
Acc. Supply $8	4.0	2.8	0.9	1.2	-2.3	3.0	2.3	1.9	0.9	1.0	-0.5	-0.6	0.4
Acc. S/Con. $8	4.2	3.3	0.5	1.1	0.6	2.8	2.2	1.2	0.5	0.1	-0.8	-1.0	0.1
Conservation $16	-1.6	-2.1	0.5	—	10.7	-2.8	-0.2	-0.4	0.9	1.0	1.5	1.2	0.9
Acc. S/Con. $16	0.7	-0.8	1.4	1.1	15.1	-1.3	1.5	1.0	1.8	1.9	1.7	1.2	1.6
Supply Pess. $16	-1.1	1.1	-1.8	-1.7	-20.3	1.8	-1.5	-1.5	-2.0	-2.5	-2.1	-1.7	-2.0

Occupation Impacts

	Professional, Technical and Kindred Workers	Managers Officials and Proprietors	Sales Workers	Clerical Workers	Crafts and Kindred Workers	Operatives	Service Workers	Nonfarm Laborers	Farmers and Farm Workers
Actual Change									
Conservation $8	-59	-27	-40	-80	126	113	-100	21	9
Acc. Supply $8	32	75	53	86	198	233	6	54	21
Acc. S/Con. $8	-1	26	3	14	166	194	-46	38	19
Conservation $16	86	63	63	132	-33	29	99	2	-1
Acc. S/Con. $16	145	140	120	242	110	215	139	45	19
Supply Pess. $16	-188	-177	-152	-309	-125	-248	-188	-55	-29
Percent Change									
Conservation $8	-0.6	-0.3	-0.6	-0.5	1.1	0.9	-1.1	0.6	0.5
Acc. Supply $8	0.3	0.8	0.8	0.5	1.8	1.8	0.1	1.5	1.2
Acc. S/Con. $8	—	0.3	—	0.1	1.5	1.5	-0.5	1.0	1.1
Conservation $16	0.8	0.7	0.9	0.8	-0.3	0.2	1.0	0.1	—
Acc. S/Con. $16	1.4	1.5	1.8	1.5	1.0	1.6	1.5	1.2	1.1
Supply Pess. $16	-1.8	-1.9	-2.3	-2.0	-1.1	-1.9	-2.0	-1.5	-1.7

Source: Authors' estimates.
Note: Impacts are shown in thousands of jobs relative to the Reference $13 scenario.

Simultaneous changes in the world price of crude oil and domestic energy policy have smaller impacts on employment in the private economy relative to the Reference $13 scenario when the world price of crude oil falls to $8 than when it rises to $16. This pattern holds for the introduction of conservation, changes in domestic energy supply conditions, and changes in both domestic energy supply and demand conditions. Although real GNP changes substantially when the world price of crude oil falls to $8, productivity changes in the same direction largely offset potential employment impacts. Real GNP does not change as much when the world price of crude oil rises to $16, but productivity changes in the opposite direction magnify the employment impacts in two cases, and a productivity change in the same direction more than offsets the real GNP related employment impact in the other case.

The Conservation $8 scenario and the Conservation $16 scenario combine a change in the world price of crude oil with the introduction of conservation. With both scenarios employment in the private economy changes in the opposite direction than would be expected on the basis of the sums of the relevant impacts reported in Tables 9-1 and 9-2. The changes in employment are relatively small with both scenarios, reflecting changes in productivity similar to the changes in real GNP. Relative to the Reference $13 scenario, employment in the private economy is lower by 37,000 jobs, a negligible percent difference, with the Conservation $8 scenario, and higher by 440,000 jobs, a 0.5 percent difference, with the Conservation $16 scenario.

Employment gains and losses for the ten major sectors total 536,000 and 573,000 jobs, respectively, for the Conservation $8 scenario and 621,000 and 181,000 jobs, respectively, with the Conservation $16 scenario. Manufacturing and Construction gain the most jobs with the Conservation $8 scenario and lose the most jobs with the Conservation $16 scenario, while Services and Wholesale and Retail Trade lose the most jobs with the former and gain the most jobs with the latter. Mining experiences by far the largest employment impact in percent terms with both scenarios. Domestic production of coal, natural gas, and crude oil is lower by 10.6 percent, 8.2 percent, and 19.9 percent, respectively, with the Conservation $8 scenario. The average of these production changes is larger than the Mining employment reduction of 7.6 percent for that scenario, because an increase in real GNP keeps the Mining employment reduction at a minimum. Domestic production of coal and crude oil is higher by 5.4 percent and 8.9 percent, respectively, with the Conservation $16 scenario, while domestic production of natural gas is lower by 0.3 percent. The Mining employment rise of 10.7 percent for this scenario is inconsistent with both the average of these production changes and the lower real GNP for the scenario. Four of the nine major occupations gain jobs, and the five others lose jobs with the Conservation $8 scenario, whereas all but two major sectors gain jobs with the Conservation $16 scenario.

The Accelerated Supply $8 scenario and the Supply Pessimism $16 scenario combine changes in the world price of crude oil and domestic energy supply conditions. Relative to the Reference $13 scenario, employment in the private economy is higher by 758,000 jobs, a 0.9 percent difference, with the Accelerated Supply $8 scenario, and lower by 1,471,000, a -1.8 percent difference, with the Supply Pessimism $16 scenario. Both of these impacts are in the direction that would be expected on the basis of the sums of the relevant impacts reported in Tables 9-1 and 9-2 for the two types of change considered separately. The positive impact for the Accelerated Supply $8 scenario is smaller than the sum of the relevant separate impacts, while the negative impact for the Supply Pessimism $16 scenario is larger than the sum of the relevant separate impacts.

Employment gains and losses for the ten major sectors total 924,000 and 166,000 jobs, respectively, with the Accelerated Supply $8 scenario and 89,000 and 1,560,000 jobs, respectively, with the Supply Pessimism $16 scenario. Manufacturing, Wholesale and Retail Trade, and Construction gain the most jobs with the Accelerated Supply $8 scenario, while Services loses the most jobs. All major sectors except Construction lose jobs with the Supply Pessimism $16 scenario, Wholesale and Retail Trade losing by far the most jobs. Construction and Manufacturing gain the most employment in percent terms, and Mining loses the most employment in percent terms with the Accelerated Supply $8 scenario. Mining loses eight times more employment than any other major sector in percent terms with the Supply Pessimism $16 scenario. Domestic production of coal and crude oil is lower by 11.0 percent and 7.0 percent, respectively, and that of natural gas is higher by 6.8 percent with the Accelerated Supply $8 scenario. Domestic production of coal, natural gas, and crude oil is lower by 7.8 percent, 19.5 percent, and 30.8 percent, respectively, with the Supply Pessimism $16 scenario. The averages of these two sets of production changes are consistent with the Mining employment reductions of 2.3 percent in the Accelerated Supply $8 scenario and 20.3 percent in the Supply Pessimism $16 scenario. Employment is higher in all nine major occupations with the Accelerated Supply $8 scenario and lower in all of them with the Supply Pessimism $16 scenario.

The Accelerated Supply and Conservation $8 scenario and the Accelerated Supply and Conservation $16 scenario combine a change in the world price of crude oil with changes in both domestic energy demand and supply conditions. Relative to the Reference $13 scenario, employment in the private economy is higher by 413,000 jobs, a 0.5 percent difference, with the Accelerated Supply and Conservation $8 scenario, and higher by 1,175,000 jobs, a 1.4 percent difference, with the Accelerated Supply and Conservation $16 scenario. Both of these positive impacts would be expected on the basis of the relevant sums of impacts reported in Tables 9-1 and 9-2 for the two types of change considered separately. The impact for the Accelerated Supply and Conservation $8 scenario is smaller than the sum of the relevant separate impacts, while the impact for the Accelerated Supply and Conservation $16 scenario is larger than the sum of the relevant separate impacts.

Employment gains and losses for the ten major sectors total 657,000 and 244,000 jobs, respectively, for the Accelerated Supply and Conservation $8 scenario and 1,239,000 and 64,000 jobs, respectively, for the Accelerated Supply and Conservation $16 scenario. Manufacturing and Construction gain the most jobs with the Accelerated Supply and Conservation $8 scenario, with only two major sectors losing jobs. Wholesale and Retail Trade, Manufacturing, and Services gain the most jobs with the Accelerated Supply and Conservation $16 scenario, with only Construction losing jobs. Construction and Manufacturing gain the most employment in percent terms with the Accelerated Supply and Conservation $8 scenario, while Mining gains eight times more employment than any other major sector in percent terms with the Accelerated Supply and Conservation $16 scenario. Domestic production of coal and crude oil is lower by 5.5 percent and 7.2 percent, respectively, and that of natural gas is higher by 4.2 percent with the Accelerated Supply and Conservation $8 scenario. Domestic production of coal is lower by 2.1 percent, and that of natural gas and crude oil is higher by 11.0 percent and 24.3 percent, respectively, with the Accelerated Supply and Conservation $16 scenario. The averages of these two sets of production impacts are broadly consistent with the 0.6 percent higher Mining employment with the Accelerated Supply and Conservation $8 scenario and the 15.1 percent higher Mining employment with the Accelerated Supply and Conservation $16 scenario. Employment is higher in all but two major occupations with the Accelerated Supply and Conservation $8 scenario and higher for all nine major occupations with the Accelerated Supply and Conservation $16 scenario.

Summary and Conclusions

For the most part the impacts on employment in the private economy reported in this chapter are not as large as the impacts on real GNP. Changes in productivity in the same direction as the changes in real GNP typically offset the potential employment impacts. Employment in the private economy tends to change less when the world price of crude oil changes than when domestic energy policy changes. Productivity, which is a function of private real GNP and the gross effective capital stock, changes more when the world price of crude oil changes, dampening the potential employment impact. The elasticity of employment in the private economy with respect to the world price of crude oil is higher for increases in the world price of crude oil to $16 than for decreases in it to $8. This pattern holds whether changes in the world price of crude oil are considered in isolation or in combination with changes in domestic energy policy. Simultaneous changes in the world price of crude oil and domestic energy policy cause employment impacts which diverge from the summed impacts of the two types of change considered separately.

The major sectors and occupations experience offsetting employment impacts when the world price of crude oil changes, whereas they tend to experience impacts in the same direction when domestic energy policy changes. Two or three major sectors absorb a disproportionate share of the impact on employment in the private economy with every scenario considered. The major occupations share the impacts more evenly, reflecting demands for a mix of skills in all major sectors. PIES domestic energy production constraints are not incorporated into the simulation procedure. Thus, Mining employment changes to satisfy final demand as derived through DRI model simulations. Nevertheless, for most scenarios the Mining employment impacts are consistent with PIES information.

The simulation procedure outlined in this chapter provides an analytical tool that is useful in forecasting the employment impacts of alternative energy futures in considerable detail. Nevertheless, improvements in the current procedure are needed both to develop an I-O model structured from an energy perspective and to link the model to other models in a more satisfactory manner. In the past data limitations have necessitated treating energy with a high degree of aggregation. New energy consumption data now being collected on an industry-by-industry basis will soon make it feasible to treat energy on a more disaggregated basis in the I-O model. However, a more disaggregated bridge table from final demand to the I-O model, a better method of dealing with productivity changes across scenarios, and some means of allowing for substitution among inputs across scenarios are also needed. Finally the establishment of feedback mechanisms from the I-O model to the demand side of PIES and the DRI model are highly desirable.

References

1. Federal Energy Administration. *National Energy Outlook* (Washington, D.C.: U.S. Government Printing Office, 1976).

2. Kutscher, Ronald E.. "Revised BLS Projections to 1980 and 1985: An Overview." *Monthly Labor Review*, 99, no. 3 (March 1976), pp. 3-8.

3. U.S. Department of Labor, Bureau of Labor Statistics. *The Structure of the U.S. Economy in 1980 and 1985* (Washington, D.C.: U.S. Government Printing Office, 1975).

10 Regional Economic Implications of National Energy Scenarios
A. David Sandoval and *Robert M. Schnapp*

Introduction

This chapter examines the implications of alternative energy scenarios for the economies of the fifty states and the District of Columbia. Scenarios developed by the Federal Energy Administration (FEA) for *Project Independence Report* and *National Energy Outlook* are analyzed with two different versions of a regional impact modeling system to determine 1985 state earnings levels for alternative domestic energy policies and world prices of crude oil.[a]

The chapter contains three main sections. The first section presents the two versions of the modeling system used to estimate the state economic impacts. The second section briefly describes the energy scenarios considered and reports the state economic impacts implied by those scenarios. Special attention is given to those states expected to be particularly sensitive to changes in energy supply or demand. The last section interprets the results obtained with the two different versions of the modeling system and examines the policy implications of the analysis.

Methodology

Figure 10-1 shows the major components of the Regional Earnings Impact System (REIS), which uses differential growth rates in thirty-seven sectors of the economy at the national level and state differences in the composition of those sectors to estimate the state earnings impacts of energy events. The REIS consists of the Project Independence Evaluation System (PIES) energy sector model, a macroeconomic model, an I-O model, and a regional distribution model. Output from one model serves as input into another in a recursive solution process. PIES consists of an econometric demand model, linear constraint supply models, and a fixed point programming model which determines market clearing prices and quantities for energy products.[b] The equilibrium conditions are designed to satisfy the demand for energy at minimum average cost. Each solution describes a static market equilibrium for some scenario in a given year.

---

[a]See [3] and [4].

[b]For a description of PIES, see appendix A in [4].

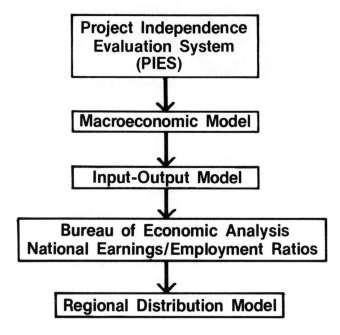

Figure 10-1. Flow Chart of the Regional Earnings Impact System

Given energy prices and quantities from PIES for an energy scenario, the implied impacts on the national economy are determined with a macroeconometric model. Components of final demand from the macroeconometric model are then entered into an I-O model to generate employment estimates for individual sectors of the economy. The individual sector employment projections from the I-O model are next aggregated into earnings estimates for thirty-seven sectors of the economy, based on trends extrapolated from historical relationships, with Bureau of Economic Analysis (BEA) earnings-to-employment ratios. These earnings estimates are used to drive the regional distribution model.

The regional distribution model determines state earnings with economic base theory on the assumption that industries are either basic or residentiary.[c] Basic industries generate economic activity within a state through exports of goods and services to other states. Residentiary industries satisfy mainly local demands within the state. Using economic projections developed jointly by the BEA and the Economic Research Service in the U.S. Department of Agriculture for the thirty-seven BEA sectors mentioned above, the regional distribution

---

[c]The earnings estimates represent the sum of wages and salaries, proprietors' income, and other labor income. Many consider earnings to be the best measure of economic activity currently available at the regional level. For an introductory discussion of economic base theory, see [5, pp. 182-231, 621-37].

model estimates the level of basic industrial activity within each state, the multiplier effects on residentiary industrial activity within each state, and the level of earnings within each state.[d]

Two different versions of the REIS were used in this chapter. The Chase version used the Chase Econometric Associates, Inc. (Chase) macroeconometric model and the Inforum I-O model.[e] The DRI version used the DRI macroeconometric model and the BLS I-O model.[f]

In the Chase version of the REIS, the analysis was begun by using PIES information to calculate a vector of energy price indexes. Differences in this vector across scenarios were multiplied by the $(I-A)^{-1}$ matrix for the Inforum I-O model to estimate price changes across scenarios for all sectors of that model. The implied sector price changes were translated into the appropriate implicit price deflator changes for use in the Chase model with a set of bridge equations. The Chase model was simulated using these implicit price deflator changes in combination with energy sector import and investment changes generated from additional PIES data. Components of final demand from the Chase model simulations were fed back into the Inforum I-O model to generate employment estimates for ninety-six sectors. These employment estimates were aggregated to the thirty-seven BEA sectors and multiplied by the BEA earnings-to-employment ratios to produce the input required for the regional distribution model.

In the DRI version of the REIS, PIES energy prices, quantities, and imports were fed directly into simulations of the DRI model. This approach did not use as many inputs from PIES as does the Chase version. Nineteen components of final demand from these simulations were entered into the BLS I-O model to generate employment estimates for 129 sectors. The employment estimates were aggregated to thirty-four of the thirty-seven BEA sectors and used in conjunction with standard BEA employment projections for the other three sectors. Standard BEA projections of federal government, state and local government, and armed forces employment were used in all scenarios, because the BLS I-O model generates employment estimates only for the private economy. The resulting employment estimates for the thirty-seven BEA sectors were multiplied by the BEA earnings-to-employment ratios to produce the input required for the regional distribution model.

---

[d]For a description of the thirty-seven BEA sectors economic projections methodology, see [6]. For a discussion of the projections, see [7].

[e]The linkages between PIES, the Chase model and the Inforum I-O model are described in [2]. Inforum is a dynamic, I-O forecasting system developed at the University of Maryland. It is described in [1].

[f]The linkages between PIES and the DRI model are discussed in Chapter 7 of this volume. The linkages between the DRI model and the BLS I-O model are discussed in Chapter 9 of this volume. The productivity adjustments developed by Earley and Mohtadi were not completed at the time this study was undertaken.

Regional Impacts

The energy scenarios postulated for *Project Independence Report* and *National Energy Outlook* consider the 1985 energy sector implications of changes in both domestic energy policy and the world price of crude oil. Four scenarios from *Project Independence Report* were selected for analysis with the Chase version of the REIS: Business as Usual $11, Business as Usual $7, Conservation $11, Accelerated Supply and Conservation $11. The dollar figures associated with the four scenarios represent the 1985 world prices of crude oil assumed to exist, as measured in 1973 constant dollars. Four comparable scenarios from *National Energy Outlook* were selected for analysis with the DRI version of the REIS: Reference $13, Reference $8, Conservation $13, Accelerated Supply and Conservation $13. The dollar figures associated with these four scenarios represent the 1985 world prices of crude oil assumed to exist, as measured in 1975 constant dollars.

The two sets of scenarios form four pairs of roughly equivalent scenarios in which the world price of crude oil is measured in different terms.[g] The Business as Usual and Reference scenarios represent a continuation of the status quo with respect to domestic energy policy. The Conservation scenarios assume a national effort to achieve energy independence through nonprice conservation measures that reduce energy consumption. The Accelerated Supply and Conservation scenarios assume efforts to expand domestic energy production in addition to the demand side measures of the Conservation scenarios.[h] All scenarios assume unlimited availability of foreign oil at the specified price. The $11 price in 1973 constant dollars and the $13 price in 1975 constant dollars approximate the actual world prices of crude oil in effect during 1974 and 1976, respectively, when the two sets of scenarios were developed.

---

[g]The two sets of scenarios differ with respect to their levels of energy consumption and the differences in these levels across scenarios. Total 1985 energy consumption is 103 quadrillion Btu with the Business as Usual $11 secnario, 109 quadrillion Btu with the Business as Usual $7 scenario, 94 quadrillion Btu with the Conservation $11 scenario, 96 quadrillion Btu with the Accelerated Supply and Conservation $11 scenario. Total 1985 energy consumption is 99 quadrillion Btu with the Reference $13 scenario, 103 quadrillion Btu with the Reference $8 scenario, 93 quadrillion Btu with the Conservation $13 scenario, and 96 quadrillion Btu with the Conservation and Accelerated Supply $13 scenario. The two sets of scenarios are more volatile with respect to the demand and supply for individual fuels, of course. See [3] and [4].

[h]Expanded domestic energy production assumes enhanced resource development involving improved oil and gas finding rates, expanded nuclear electricity generation, expanded Alaskan oil and gas supplies, and expanded commercial development of solar, geothermal, and synthetic energy resources. Specific conservation actions include auto efficiency standards, car and van pooling, thermal efficiency standards, appliance efficiency improvements, accelerated industrial energy conservation, airline load factor increases, electric utility load management, and gas pilot light elimination.

The Chase Version Results

Table 10-1 shows the direct and total 1985 earnings effects of the other three *Project Independence Report* scenarios relative to the Business as Usual $11 scenario as estimated with the Chase version of the REIS. The direct effects reflect a simple allocation of national earnings for each of the thirty-seven BEA sectors to the individual states. The total effects include multiplier effects on residentiary industries based on a national classification of basic versus residentiary industries.

Considering direct effects, thirty states have higher 1985 earnings, and twenty states plus the District of Columbia have lower 1985 earning with the Business as Usual $7 scenario than with the Business as Usual $11 scenario. The mean direct effect on 1985 earnings is -0.08 percent, however, because negative impacts to the major energy-producing states of Alaska, Louisiana, Oklahoma, Texas, West Virginia, and Wyoming outweigh modest gains elsewhere. The states with the largest gains are major producers of consumer-oriented goods that benefit from a higher level of national economic activity. Such states include Indiana, Michigan, North Carolina, and South Carolina. Considering total effects, thirty-five states have higher 1985 earnings, and fifteen states plus the District of Columbia have lower 1985 earnings. The mean total effect on 1985 earnings is -0.13 percent. In most cases, positive or negative direct effects are accentuated by secondary effects, but there are five exceptions. Negative direct effects in California, Florida, Maryland, Nevada, and Virginia become positive total effects when residentiary multiplier effects are considered, because service activities which benefit from lower energy prices are very important to these states.

All states and the District of Columbia have lower 1985 earnings with the Conservation $11 scenario than with the Business as Usual $11 scenario, reflecting a slightly lower level of national economic activity associated with energy conservation. This outcome holds for both direct and total effects. The mean direct and total effects on 1985 earnings are -0.63 percent and -0.64 percent, respectively. The states most affected by conservation measures are the major domestic energy producers. The 1985 earnings in Kentucky, Louisiana, Oklahoma, Pennsylvania, Texas, West Virginia, and Wyoming are lower because of lower domestic oil and coal production.

Considering direct effects, all states and the District of Columbia have lower 1985 earnings with the Accelerated Supply and Conservation $11 scenario than with the Business as Usual $11 scenario. The mean direct effect on 1985 earnings is -0.61 percent. The 1985 earnings in West Virginia are 2.14 percent lower because of the substantially lower level of coal consumption. The 1985 earnings in Kentucky, Ohio, and Pennsylvania are similarly affected. The 1985 earnings in Ohio are also affected by reduced automobile production, as they are in Michigan and Indiana, reflecting a lower national level of economic activity. Considering total effects, six states plus the District of Columbia have higher 1985 earnings. The mean total effect on 1985 earnings is -0.52 percent. Alaska, Louisiana, Texas, and Wyoming are energy-producing states. North Dakota and the District of Columbia have higher 1985 earnings because of the presence of agriculture in North Dakota, the federal government in the District of Columbia, and the lack of manufacturing, an adversely affected industry, in both areas.

The DRI Version Results

Table 10-2 shows the direct and total 1985 earnings effects of the other three *National Energy Outlook* scenarios relative to the Reference $13 scenario as estimated with the DRI version of the REIS. The total effects reflect a state-by-state classification of basic versus residentiary industries.

Considering direct effects, all states and the District of Columbia have higher 1985 earnings with the Reference $8 scenario than with the Reference $13 scenario. The mean direct effect on 1985 earnings is 2.64 percent. The states with the largest gains are major producers of manufactured goods that benefit from lower costs and a higher level of national economic activity. Such states include Connecticut, Indiana, Michigan, and Ohio. The 1985 earnings in the energy-producing states of Alaska, Louisiana, New Mexico, Oklahoma, West Virginia, and Wyoming experience the smallest impacts. Considering total effects, three states and the District of Columbia have lower 1985 earnings. The mean total effect on 1985 earnings is 2.37 percent. Louisiana, West Virigina, and Wyoming have lower 1985 earnings, because lower energy production results in adverse multiplier effects. The District of Columbia has lower 1985 earnings, because it depends on government employment that remains constant across scenarios. The 1985 earnings in Michigan and Indiana are more than 5 percent higher when multiplier effects are considered, reflecting a higher level of national economic activity that helps automobile production.

Considering direct effects, all states and the District of Columbia have lower 1985 earnings with the Conservation $13 scenario than with the Reference $13 scenario. The mean direct effect on 1985 earnings is just -0.06 percent, however, and only the two coal producing states of Kentucky and West Virginia experience 1985 earnings losses of more than -0.1 percent. Considering total effects, seven states plus the District of Columbia have marginally higher 1985 earnings. The mean total effect on 1985 earnings remains virtually unchanged at -0.07 percent. No state gains more than 0.02 percent in 1985 earnings.

Considering direct effects, twenty-nine states have higher 1985 earnings, and twenty-one states plus the District of Columbia have lower 1985 earnings with the Accelerated Supply and Conservation $13 scenario than with the Reference $13 scenario. The mean direct effect on 1985 earnings is 0.05 percent. West Virginia loses the most 1985 earnings—-0.2 percent—because of lower coal production, while the oil producing states gain the most. Positive direct ef-

Table 10–1
Project Independence Report Earnings Comparisons for 1985

State	Business as Usual $7				Conservation $11				Accelerated Supply Conservation $11			
	Direct Effect		Total Effect		Direct Effect		Total Effect		Direct Effect		Total Effect	
	Dollar Change	*Percent Change*	*Dollar Change*	*Percent Change*	*Dollar Change*	*Percent Change*	*Dollar Change*	*Percent Change*	*Dollar Change*	*Percent Change*	*Dollar Change*	*Percent Change*
Alabama	5958.00	0.05	13395.00	0.10	- 88058.00	-0.64	- 85879.00	-0.62	-100368.00	-0.73	-104605.00	-0.76
Alaska	- 17613.00	-0.75	- 32357.00	-1.31	- 15928.00	-0.68	- 17174.00	-0.69	- 1846.00	-0.07	10745.00	0.44
Arizona	6681.00	0.07	24538.00	0.25	- 75628.00	-0.75	- 89053.00	-0.87	- 73738.00	-0.73	- 83267.00	-0.81
Arkansas	5110.00	0.08	10705.00	0.16	- 41226.00	-0.59	- 35051.00	-0.51	- 37511.00	-0.53	- 26675.00	-0.39
California	- 11328.00	-0.00	6113.00	0.01	-771376.00	-0.66	-769696.00	-0.66	-710144.00	-0.61	-640064.00	-0.55
Colorado	- 25973.00	-0.20	- 54325.00	-0.43	- 84396.00	-0.68	- 88479.00	-0.70	- 62950.00	-0.50	- 37651.00	-0.29
Connecticut	5409.00	0.04	- 23361.00	0.14	-128000.00	-0.73	-141744.00	-0.83	-141296.00	-0.81	-169044.00	-0.99
Delaware	3583.00	0.11	8658.00	0.27	- 13881.00	-0.41	- 6058.00	-0.18	- 22297.00	-0.65	- 20440.00	-0.62
D.C.	- 2773.00	-0.02	- 7485.00	-0.05	- 37417.00	-0.31	- 7526.00	-0.05	- 28550.00	-0.24	15698.00	0.13
Florida	- 16160.00	-0.04	4353.00	0.02	-223888.00	-0.60	-193680.00	-0.51	-194688.00	-0.52	-134704.00	-0.35
Georgia	22289.00	0.10	52561.00	0.24	-125104.00	-0.55	- 92352.00	-0.40	- 13308.00	-0.58	-109840.00	-0.48
Hawaii	- 4094.00	-0.08	- 5269.00	-0.10	- 23551.00	-0.47	- 12265.00	-0.23	- 18393.00	-0.37	- 528.00	-0.01
Idaho	2678.00	0.10	6608.00	0.24	- 12682.00	-0.44	- 5672.00	-0.19	- 11557.00	-0.40	- 2652.00	-0.09
Illinois	5649.00	0.01	44913.00	0.08	-466416.00	-0.73	-507392.00	-0.81	-503584.00	-0.79	-590592.00	-0.94
Indiana	34945.00	0.14	72065.00	0.28	-188272.00	-0.70	-192192.00	-0.72	-263904.00	-0.98	-323776.00	-1.22
Iowa	3039.00	0.03	9066.00	0.08	- 70779.00	-0.58	- 58448.00	-0.48	- 73635.00	-0.60	- 61633.00	-0.51
Kansas	- 14125.00	-0.15	- 26547.00	-0.29	- 53213.00	-0.59	- 45534.00	-0.51	- 42815.00	-0.47	- 23454.00	-0.26
Kentucky	- 23490.00	-0.17	- 39623.00	-0.29	-111745.00	-0.81	-129566.00	-0.95	-151829.00	-1.10	-203804.00	-1.49
Louisiana	-145487.00	-1.05	-324936.00	-2.34	-133494.00	-0.97	-187672.00	-1.35	- 4007.00	-0.02	107627.00	-0.78
Maine	4275.00	0.12	9731.00	0.27	- 20270.00	-0.55	- 15947.00	-0.44	- 20265.00	-0.55	- 15064.00	-0.41
Maryland	- 2176.00	-0.01	6625.00	0.03	-118304.00	-0.55	- 96176.00	-0.43	-124064.00	-0.58	-102928.00	-0.46
Massachusetts	11905.00	0.04	50385.00	0.17	-215504.00	-0.69	-228672.00	-0.74	-214352.00	-0.68	-234416.00	-0.76
Michigan	68273.00	0.14	130081.00	0.26	-171744.00	-0.33	- 33632.00	-0.06	-552192.00	-1.08	-711984.00	-1.37
Minnesota	4145.00	0.03	19809.00	0.11	-133056.00	-0.67	-134080.00	-0.68	-135792.00	-0.68	-139392.00	-0.71
Mississippi	- 4865.00	-0.06	- 7919.00	-0.10	- 46195.00	-0.62	- 42796.00	-0.58	- 37109.00	-0.50	- 24008.00	-0.32
Missouri	16497.00	0.08	43729.00	0.19	-137760.00	-0.59	-112096.00	-0.48	-165600.00	-0.71	-176848.00	-0.76
Montana	- 1824.00	-0.06	- 3028.00	-0.11	- 15269.00	-0.57	- 12836.00	-0.47	- 10749.00	-0.40	- 2999.00	-0.11
Nebraska	962.00	0.02	4030.00	0.07	- 35641.00	-0.54	- 25350.00	-0.39	- 32562.00	-0.49	- 18938.00	-0.29
Nevada	- 1628.00	-0.04	1834.00	0.05	- 22602.00	-0.61	- 21941.00	-0.55	- 18309.00	-0.49	- 12038.00	-0.30
New Hampshire	3150.00	0.10	9482.00	0.29	- 24459.00	-0.72	- 26399.00	-0.80	- 24399.00	-0.71	- 26087.00	-0.79
New Jersey	29041.00	0.08	90961.00	0.24	-278800.00	-0.68	-282944.00	-0.71	-274976.00	-0.67	-285568.00	-0.72
New Mexico	- 15634.00	-0.37	- 32852.00	-0.74	- 30992.00	-0.74	- 36329.00	-0.82	- 15502.00	-0.37	- 1025.00	-0.02
New York	35601.00	0.04	126961.00	0.12	-744464.00	-0.68	-785376.00	-0.72	-711872.00	-0.65	-757080.00	-0.69
North Carolina	40961.00	0.18	81041.00	0.36	-139488.00	-0.60	-121392.00	-0.53	-146320.00	-0.63	-128320.00	-0.56
North Dakota	- 3083.00	-0.14	- 5925.00	-0.27	- 10067.00	-0.47	- 5592.00	-0.26	- 7292.00	-0.34	667.00	0.04
Ohio	36849.00	0.07	88561.00	0.16	-385952.00	-0.68	-386832.00	-0.69	-531408.00	-0.93	-663936.00	-1.18
Oklahoma	- 87282.00	-0.81	-178298.00	-1.62	- 94423.00	-0.87	-118697.00	-1.08	- 21430.00	-0.19	33454.00	0.31
Oregon	12704.00	0.13	31156.00	0.30	- 55051.00	-0.53	- 37384.00	-0.35	- 56264.00	-0.54	- 40030.00	-0.38
Pennsylvania	18449.00	0.04	60289.00	0.11	-457664.00	-0.79	-532992.00	-0.93	-530448.00	-0.91	-683920.00	-1.19
Rhode Island	4073.00	0.09	10111.00	0.22	- 29619.00	-0.63	- 27962.00	-0.60	- 31134.00	-0.66	- 29881.00	-0.64
South Carolina	14022.00	0.14	28323.00	0.28	- 61364.00	-0.58	- 52909.00	-0.51	- 64401.00	-0.61	- 54502.00	-0.52
South Dakota	1286.00	0.06	2331.00	0.10	- 10291.00	-0.43	- 5058.00	-0.21	- 8987.00	-0.38	- 1676.00	-0.07
Tennessee	21185.00	0.12	47153.00	0.27	-117312.00	-0.65	-112992.00	-0.64	-125568.00	-0.70	-125168.00	-0.71
Texas	-275168.00	-0.51	-604016.00	-1.13	-429632.00	-0.80	-522912.00	-0.98	-179952.00	-0.33	45841.00	0.09
Utah	- 2495.00	-0.04	- 4474.00	-0.08	- 34612.00	-0.68	- 36868.00	-0.70	- 31582.00	-0.62	- 29319.00	-0.55
Vermont	1255.00	0.07	4694.00	0.24	- 14619.00	-0.71	- 15847.00	-0.80	- 13828.00	-0.67	- 14223.00	-0.71
Virginia	- 3808.00	-0.01	- 192.00	0.00	-132192.00	-0.57	-113200.00	-0.48	-143632.00	-0.62	-128512.00	-0.54
Washington	4509.00	0.03	16049.00	0.10	- 95872.00	-0.57	- 78272.00	-0.46	- 95351.00	-0.56	- 74752.00	-0.43
West Virginia	- 52744.00	-0.81	- 98322.00	-1.50	- 86652.00	-1.33	-127137.00	-1.94	-139677.00	-2.14	-229321.00	-3.50
Wisconsin	12497.00	0.07	29153.00	0.15	-133104.00	-0.64	-125856.00	-0.61	-168016.00	-0.80	-188112.00	-0.91
Wyoming	- 17696.00	-1.22	- 35850.00	-2.41	- 15641.00	-1.08	- 22516.00	-1.51	- 301.00	-0.02	9602.00	0.65

Source: Authors' estimates.

Note: All effects are stated in thousands of 1967 dollars relative to the Business as Usual $11 Scenario effects.

Table 10-2

National Energy Outlook Earnings Comparison for 1985

State	Reference $8				Conservation $13				Accelerated Supply/Conservation $13			
	Direct Effect		Total Effect		Direct Effect		Total Effect		Direct Effect		Total Effect	
	Dollar Change	Percent Change	Dollar Change	Percent Change	Dollar Change	Percent Change	Dollar Change	Percent Change	Dollar Change	Percent Change	Dollar Change	Percent Change
Alabama	320606.00	2.69	304599.00	2.53	-7407.00	-0.06	-7332.00	-0.06	1351.00	0.01	-2548.00	-0.02
Alaska	28436.00	1.44	9213.00	0.46	-837.00	-0.04	-565.00	-0.03	6752.00	0.34	11335.00	0.56
Arizona	249508.00	2.80	251899.00	2.76	-5242.00	-0.06	-4286.00	-0.05	-3012.00	-0.03	-23496.00	-0.26
Arkansas	180630.00	2.93	194595.00	3.25	-3579.00	-0.06	-2803.00	-0.05	3565.00	0.06	6783.00	0.11
California	2740067.00	2.68	2201923.00	2.10	-63539.00	-0.06	-63841.00	-0.06	13884.00	0.01	-67289.00	-0.06
Colorado	265310.00	2.44	82619.00	0.71	-7105.00	-0.07	-9655.00	-0.08	12917.00	0.12	56272.00	0.48
Connecticut	504528.00	3.21	672074.00	4.27	-7042.00	-0.04	-475.00	0.00	-2275.00	-0.01	-20879.00	-0.13
Delaware	88874.00	3.09	98268.00	3.93	-1478.00	-0.05	-481.00	-0.02	-687.00	-0.02	-2751.00	-0.11
D.C.	135981.00	1.38	-33941.00	-0.33	-3156.00	-0.03	-585.00	0.01	-1400.00	-0.01	-7585.00	-0.07
Florida	868264.00	2.65	637458.00	1.80	-25186.00	-0.08	-49020.00	-0.14	-5089.00	-0.03	-111285.00	-0.31
Georgia	537990.00	2.68	483467.00	2.36	-12955.00	-0.06	-14282.00	-0.07	-2998.00	-0.07	-1805.00	-0.01
Hawaii	89342.00	2.07	35408.00	0.78	-3080.00	-0.07	-4025.00	-0.09	-276.00	-0.01	-11880.00	-0.26
Idaho	71158.00	2.86	75503.00	3.04	-1810.00	-0.07	-2490.00	-0.10	-3530.00	-0.02	-3226.00	-0.13
Illinois	1777908.00	3.15	2305705.00	4.18	-39686.00	-0.07	-49555.00	-0.09	-11960.00	-0.02	-89882.00	-0.13
Indiana	836807.00	3.59	1139312.00	5.16	-13592.00	-0.06	-10316.00	-0.05	-861.00	-0.01	-21102.00	-0.10
Iowa	324896.00	3.04	377612.00	3.61	-7518.00	-0.07	-8948.00	-0.07	5955.00	0.08	-9771.00	-0.09
Kansas	202899.00	2.58	149902.00	1.92	-5101.00	-0.06	-5582.00	-0.07	-7573.00	-0.06	17466.00	0.22
Kentucky	317951.00	2.63	275328.00	2.34	-16027.00	-0.13	-26630.00	-0.28	74630.00	0.62	-29981.00	-0.25
Louisiana	220310.00	1.83	-131575.00	-1.06	-6278.00	-0.05	-2620.00	-0.02	481.00	0.02	298856.00	2.36
Maine	89450.00	2.80	89499.00	2.82	-1570.00	-0.05	-201.00	-0.01	4939.00	0.02	-1028.00	-0.03
Maryland	460191.00	2.50	364191.00	1.90	-10941.00	-0.06	-10248.00	-0.05	-348.00	-0.03	-27922.00	-0.15
Massachusetts	793362.00	2.85	848980.00	3.01	-13737.00	-0.05	-2598.00	-0.01	348.00	-0.00	40565.00	0.10
Michigan	1491208.00	3.59	2041963.00	5.48	-15447.00	-0.04	-8052.00	0.02	-4141.00	-0.00	-34676.00	-0.14
Minnesota	527479.00	3.03	645077.00	3.70	-11843.00	-0.07	-14502.00	-0.08	8947.00	0.14	-32566.00	-0.19
Mississippi	178204.00	2.72	170668.00	2.61	-3060.00	-0.05	-1152.00	-0.02	1015.00	0.00	20719.00	0.32
Missouri	614668.00	2.55	746030.00	3.84	-13389.00	-0.07	-13884.00	-0.07	301.00	0.01	-14735.00	-0.08
Montana	57933.00	2.33	35628.00	1.50	-1736.00	-0.08	-2991.00	-0.13	1055.00	0.05	2261.00	0.10
Nebraska	157049.00	2.74	147134.00	2.63	-4136.00	-0.07	-5503.00	-0.10	-329.00	-0.01	3738.00	0.10
Nevada	78568.00	2.33	52165.00	1.41	-1531.00	-0.05	-714.00	-0.02	159.00	0.01	-3857.00	-0.07
New Hampshire	92977.00	3.06	116846.00	3.93	-1399.00	-0.05	-242.00	0.01	-10135.00	-0.03	-2110.00	-0.07
New Jersey	1091971.00	3.04	1315176.00	3.82	-22898.00	-0.06	-22061.00	-0.06	7317.00	0.20	-64784.00	-0.19
New Mexico	70049.00	1.95	14296.00	0.39	-2032.00	-0.06	-1679.00	-0.05	-4945.00	-0.01	19139.00	0.52
New York	2560776.00	2.67	2308761.00	2.38	-56714.00	-0.06	-48787.00	-0.05	1416.00	0.05	-86044.00	-0.09
North Carolina	606629.00	2.88	641014.00	3.03	-8261.00	-0.04	-387.00	0.00	690.00	0.01	19533.00	0.09
North Dakota	42347.00	2.29	6286.00	0.33	-1700.00	-0.09	-3810.00	-0.20	2839.00	0.01	1384.00	0.06
Ohio	1681575.00	3.41	2280281.00	4.86	-28695.00	-0.06	-21302.00	-0.05	45938.00	0.48	-20725.00	-0.04
Oklahoma	182396.00	1.93	19263.00	0.20	-4348.00	-0.05	-1400.00	-0.01	1900.00	0.02	134886.00	1.38
Oregon	279080.00	3.07	367665.00	3.92	-5146.00	-0.06	-3392.00	-0.04	-15332.00	-0.03	-1745.00	-0.02
Pennsylvania	1573076.00	3.08	1941551.00	3.85	-37357.00	-0.07	-50365.00	-0.10	778.00	0.02	-94848.00	-0.19
Rhode Island	112755.00	2.72	103710.00	2.46	-1751.00	-0.04	-757.00	0.02	4270.00	0.04	-828.00	-0.02
South Carolina	250943.00	2.62	226403.00	2.33	-2982.00	-0.03	-2049.00	0.02	9.00	0.00	6143.00	0.06
South Dakota	49750.00	2.42	31470.00	1.56	-1713.00	-0.08	-2706.00	-0.13	3040.00	0.02	-1534.00	-0.08
Tennessee	462815.00	2.91	506949.00	3.28	-8628.00	-0.05	-4656.00	-0.03	137932.00	0.29	-1341.00	-0.01
Texas	1113204.00	2.35	458055.00	0.93	-29191.00	-0.06	-30099.00	-0.06	1243.00	-0.03	530153.00	1.08
Utah	101147.00	3.38	64510.00	1.43	-2808.00	-0.06	-3192.00	-0.07	371.00	0.03	846.00	0.02
Vermont	55131.00	3.03	66281.00	3.74	-897.00	-0.07	-377.00	-0.08	5442.00	-0.03	-2844.00	-0.16
Virginia	466213.00	2.30	301627.00	1.46	-14690.00	-0.07	-18539.00	-0.09	3010.00	-0.02	-26945.00	-0.13
Washington	401986.00	2.72	360955.00	2.30	-9684.00	-0.07	-12619.00	-0.08	11502.00	-0.02	-34075.00	-0.22
West Virginia	86205.00	1.54	-33252.00	-0.61	-18658.00	-0.33	-44511.00	-0.82	722.00	-0.21	-33905.00	-0.62
Wisconsin	587132.00	3.24	753210.00	4.28	-9557.00	-0.05	-4987.00	-0.03		0.00	-9312.00	-0.05
Wyoming	17673.00	1.43	-21165.00	-1.64	-835.00	-0.07	-1033.00	-0.08	8168.00	0.66	26400.00	2.04

Source: Authors' estimates.

Note: All effects are stated in thousands of 1957 dollars relative to the Reference $13 scenario effects.

fects in twelve states become negative when residentiary multiplier effects are considered. The mean total effect on 1985 earnings rises to 0.09 percent, however, because larger gains in the oil producing states outweigh marginal loses in these twelve and other states.

Interpretation of the Results

The analysis of four *Project Independence Report* scenarios with the Chase version of the REIS and the analysis of four comparable *National Energy Outlook* scenarios with the DRI version of the REIS yield different results for two reasons. First, the technical details of the two versions of the REIS differ. Second, despite their similarities, the two sets of scenarios differ with respect to specific assumptions. However, the results of the two analyses are broadly consistent.

Energy-producing states do less well than other states with both analyses when foreign oil becomes cheaper. Both the direct and total 1985 state earnings effects are considerably larger and more consistently positive with the *National Energy Outlook* scenarios, reflecting a large reduction in the world price of crude oil and smaller increases in energy consumption and oil imports. The introduction of energy conservation reduces 1985 state earnings with both analyses because of a lower level of national economic activity and less energy production. The impacts are larger and more consistently negative, especially for total effects, with the *Project Independence Report* scenarios, because of larger reductions in energy consumption. Simultaneous introduction of energy conservation and acceleration of domestic energy production avoids with both analyses the adverse 1985 state earnings effects that energy conservation has by itself. The effects remain marginally negative with the *Project Independence Report* scenarios, but become marginally positive with the *National Energy Outlook* scenarios, reflecting slightly different effects on energy consumption with the two sets of scenarios.

The REIS results demonstrate clearly that energy events give rise to complex patterns of regional impacts. Some energy events affect all regions similarly, while others affect them differently. Energy conservation implies lower 1985 earnings in all states, for example, but cheaper foreign oil benefits other states at the expense of energy-producing states. In general, some states are likely to require more attention than others from national and regional decision-makers.

References

1. Almon, Clopper et al. *1985: Interindustry Forecasts of the American Economy* (Lexington, Mass.: D.C. Heath and Company, 1974).

2. Askin, A. Bradley. "The Macroeconomic Implications of Alternative Energy Scenarios." In Askin and Kraft, eds., *Econometric Dimensions of Energy*

Demand and Supply (Lexington, Mass.: D.C. Heath and Company, 1976), pp. 91–109.

3. Federal Energy Administration. *National Energy Outlook* (Washington, D.C.: U.S. Government Printing Office, 1976).

4. Federal Energy Administration. *Project Independence Report* (Washington, D.C.: U.S. Government Printing Office, 1974).

5. Isard, Walter. *Methods of Regional Analysis: An Introduction to Regional Science* (Cambridge, Mass.: The M.I.T. Press, 1960).

6. U.S. Department of Agriculture, Economic Research Service and U.S. Department of Commerce, Bureau of Economic Analysis. *1972 OBERS Projections, Vol. 1: Concepts, Methodology, and Summary Data* (Washington, D.C.: U.S. Government Printing Office, 1974).

7. U.S. Department of Commerce, Bureau of Economic Analysis. *Area Economic Projections 1990, States and Regions, BEA Economic Areas* (Washington, D.C.: U.S. Government Printing Office, 1974).

About the Contributors

Ronald F. Earley is an economist with the National Impact Division in the Office of Economic Impact Analysis at the FEA. He received the B.A. from the University of Michigan and the M.A. in economics from Miami University (Ohio) and completed further graduate studies in economics at American University.

Richard L. Farman is an economist in the National Impact Division at the FEA. He graduated from Oberlin College in 1972 with a B.A. in economics and undertook graduate training at Carnegie-Mellon University until joining Westinghouse Corporation as a corporate economist in 1975.

Gerard L. Lagace is an economist with the National Impact Division at the FEA. Previously he was an economist with the Gulf Oil Corporation and the U.S. Tariff Commission (now the International Tariff Commission). He received the B.S. and M.A. degrees from Georgetown University and the Ph.D. in economics from The George Washington University.

Arthur J. Malloy is acting chief of the Domestic Modelling and Forecasting Branch in the National Impact Division at the FEA. Prior to joining the FEA, he was an economist with the Economic Research Service at the U.S. Department of Agriculture. He is a Phi Beta Kappa graduate of the University of Connecticut and received the Ph.D. in economics from the State University of New York at Stony Brook in 1974.

Malek M. Mohtadi is an economist in the National Impact Division at the FEA. Previously he was an economist at the Census Bureau, the Price Commission, and the U.S. Department of Agriculture. He has also served on the staff of Utah State University. He is a coauthor of *World Supply and Demand Prospects for Oilseeds and Oilseed Products in 1980* and *Long-Term Projections of Selected Agricultural Products in Iran*. He holds the M.S. in economics from Utah State University.

Peter Morici, Jr. is an economist with the National Impact Division at the FEA. He was an assistant professor of economics at Augsburg College in Minneapolis before joining the FEA. He holds a B.A. from Plattsburgh State College and received the Ph.D. in economics from the State University of New York at Albany in 1974. His research and publications include work in international and energy economics.

William G. Rice is an economist with the National Impact Division at the FEA. Prior to joining the FEA he was an economist for the Cost of Living Council. He received the B.A. and M.A. in economics from Cleveland State University.

Eugene Rossidivito is an economist in the National Impact Division at the FEA. Before coming to the FEA he was chief of the Applied Economics Division, Mathematical Computations Laboratory, General Services Administration and held positions with other government agencies. He received the B.S. in economics from the University of Florida.

A. David Sandoval is an economist in the Regional Impact Division of the Office of Economic Impact Analysis at the FEA. Before coming to the FEA he was a staff economist for the Public Works Committee of the U.S. Senate. He received his Ph.D. in economics from the University of Wisconsin.

Robert M. Schnapp is an economist with the Regional Impact Division in the FEA. He holds a B.A. from the State University of New York at Binghamton and the M.A. in economics from the University of Maryland.

David E. Serot is an economist with the National Impact Division at the FEA. He received the B.A. and M.A. from the University of California at Los Angeles and the Ph.D. in economics from the University of California at Berkeley.

About the Editor

A. Bradley Askin is chief of the National Impact Division in the Office of Economic Impact Analysis at the FEA. Previously he was a federal faculty fellow at the FEA on leave from the Graduate School of Administration in the University of California at Irvine. He has also taught at Georgetown University and The George Washington University and been associated with the Rand Corporation and the Price Commission. Among his other books is *Econometric Dimensions of Energy Demand and Supply*. He holds the Ph.D. in economics from the Massachusetts Institute of Technology.